THE FOUR ELEMENTS
OF AN EMPOWERED LIFE

MOSAICA PRESS

RABBI SHLOMO BUXBAUM

THE FOUR
elements
OF AN
EMPOWERED
LIFE

A Guidebook to Discovering Your
Inner World and Unique Purpose

Published by Mosaica Press, Inc.
www.mosaicapress.com
info@mosaicapress.com

For my wife, Devorah

without whom this book and all of my endeavors
would be an impossibility. May we merit together to share
the beauty of Torah with our family, our community,
and with the entire world.

*For Meira, Shira Frayda, Moshe Mordechai,
Simcha, Daniella Chava, and Asher*

May Hashem guide each of you on the path to discover
your unique mission with the incredible gifts that you
have been given. I pray that the lessons in this book
will help you on that journey.

This book is dedicated in memory of my *rebbi*

Rabbi Mosheh Twersky
רבי משה בן ר' יצחק אשר טברסקי

Never could I have imagined how great a human being could become until I met Rabbi Twersky. I was blessed to be a guest at his Shabbos table most weeks when I was a student in Israel, and our post-meal learning sessions and conversations often went well into the late hours of the night. I will forever be grateful for having had the opportunity to spend so much time in the close presence of an angel on earth, an angel who was invited back to Heaven long before the world was ready to lose him.

With deep gratitude to all who supported this endeavor

Chaim and Miriam Buxbaum

Hadassa and Miriam Buxbaum

Doniel and Suri Czermak

Zvi and Shoshana Gelt

Nancee Gross and Mark Edelman

Erik and Connie Lindenauer

Avromi and Butchie Meyer

Rabbi Yaakov and Chaya Meyer

Dovi and Shoshana Ort

Daniel and Ilana Ratner

The Ritter Family (in honor of Gabriel)

Avi and Suri Walles

Izzy and DB Weinberg

Bob and Allison Weiss

Mike and Randy Weiss

Yossi and Ariella Zicherman

AYS Foundation
(In memory of Ari Yeruchem ben Dovid Zalman Halevi, ob"m)
The DC Momentum Men's Mastermind
Nussbaum Family Jewish Education Foundation

תפארת גדליה

YGW

From the Desk of

RABBI AHRON LOPIANSKY

Rosh HaYeshiva

Chanukah 5780

In a society filled with well-intentioned people who are scheming how to "fix the world," Rabbi Shlomo Buxbaum reminds us most powerfully that we first have to fix ourselves. Not only is this a prerequisite for healing the world but actually is the very beginning of that process. Rabbi Buxbaum uses authentic and ancient Jewish sources, drawing much on mysticism, and succeeds in translating it to a language and ideas that are accessible to the modern student.

This book is meant for the person who can seriously introspect, understand the multifaceted nature of the human, and how Torah addresses all of these various facets. It is sure to add much depth and comprehension to that person. Hopefully, we will succeed in fixing ourselves first — one facet at a time, and the world — one human being at a time!

Ahron Shraga Lopiansky

YESHIVA OF GREATER WASHINGTON - TIFERES GEDALIAH
1216 ARCOLA AVENUE, SILVER SPRING, MD 20902 ■ 301-649-7077 ■ WWW.YESHIVA.EDU

CONGREGATION ISHAY YISROEL

110 Miller Road Lakewood, New Jersey 08701 732-276-6476

Rabbi Shlomo Buxbaum's book, *The Four Elements of an Empowered Life*, hones directly in on the great desire of most Jews to have a meaningful relationship with their Judaism that is at once practical and profound. His impressive knowledge of Jewish source texts spans from basic Jewish literature to the sublimely mystical. He masterfully weaves them all together to create a fascinating armchair journey to discovery of self and G-d. I look forward eagerly to his continuing invaluable contributions to Jewish thought and growth.

Rabbi Yerachmiel Milstein,
rav, Congregation Ishay Yisroel, Lakewood, NJ;
senior lecturer,
Aish HaTorah Discovery Seminars

TABLE OF CONTENTS

Note to reader: This book weaves together both practical as well as esoteric ideas, some of which assume that the reader has some background knowledge of the Torah's narrative. In order to create an enjoyable journey for all audiences, and not lose anyone along the way, many of the Torah concepts have been placed in shaded boxes. This will make the book easier to navigate and create a point of re-entry for someone who finds the Torah concepts difficult to follow.

PREFACE

OUR SAGES TEACH that our forefather Abraham, the first of the patriarchs of the Jewish people, had an attendant and a student named Eliezer who was influential in helping spread Abraham's message to the world. He is compared by our Sages to a water-carrier, who would draw the water, i.e., the teachings, from his teacher Abraham and distribute them to the world.

In the mystical writings of the Chassidic master, the *Bnei Yissaschar*, the astrological sign of Aquarius, the water-carrier, is the sign of the Jewish People because of our mission to draw from the holy teachings of the Torah and of our Sages and distribute them to the world. This imagery has always resonated deeply with me (perhaps because I was born in the Jewish month of Shevat, the month associated with this astrological sign), but it became especially powerful as I was writing this book.

While the actual process of writing a book happens in solitude, I have found it to be a deeply connective experience. It strengthened my attachment to the many Torah sources, books, and authors upon which the ideas in the book are based. It raised my appreciation of all of the wonderful teachers and influencers that I have had the merit of benefitting from. And it helped me form a new relationship with you, the reader. Whoever and wherever you are, you were in my heart and my mind throughout this writing process.

The beautiful irony of writing a book about finding one's mission is that the book itself becomes part of the author's life mission. And, like every other aspect of one's life mission, it takes lots of soul searching, lots of enduring the highs and the lows, and lots of help from God.

I pray every day that God should help me discover my mission and that all of my endeavors should, indeed, bring me closer to that goal. I am filled with so much gratitude to the Almighty for the gift of allowing the thoughts, feelings, and words that became this book to pass through me. "My mouth shall sing much praise to Hashem; I will acclaim Him in the midst of the masses" (Psalms 109:30).

The Almighty very intentionally pairs a soul with the specific parents who have the ability to bring out his or her potential to the fullest. My parents, Chaim and Miriam Buxbaum, have been just that for me, watering and nurturing the intellectual, emotional, and creative tools that I have been given with their endless love and support.

I merited to marry into a family of world-class Jewish educators. My in-laws, Rabbi Yaakov and Chaya Meyer, built an empire in Denver, and their support, assistance, and love has propelled my personal and professional growth in so many ways.

My own spiritual journey has been supported and inspired by the wonderful institutions and holy teachers that I have been blessed to study under or receive from. As a student of Toras Moshe and the Mirrer Yeshiva of Jerusalem, I benefited from drinking from the waters of so many spiritual giants, especially my *rebbi*, the *tzaddik*, Rabbi Moshe Twerski, *zt"l*, who welcomed me as a member of his home for Shabbat for several years. I received my rabbinic ordination from Aish HaTorah, and had the benefit of catching some of the fire of the revolutionary Rabbi Noach Weinberg, *zt"l*.

The biggest blessing of living in Silver Spring, Maryland, is to be in close proximity to Rabbi Aharon Lopiansky. Since we have been here, I have had the merit to have countless conversations with the Rosh HaYeshiva and to benefit from his great wisdom. I have so much gratitude for Rav Aharon's wisdom and for his words of approbation for this work.

Much of my perception of what a relationship with God is all about has been influenced by Rav Tzvi Meir Zilberberg of Jerusalem and Rav Moshe Weinberger of New York, both of whom I do not have a personal relationship with, but have much gratitude towards. I have also benefited in my development as a teacher from the mentorship and friendship of some incredible individuals who are making their mark on the Jewish world, including Rabbi Doniel Katz, Rabbi Dov Ber Cohen, Rabbi Yeruchum Goldwasser, and Charlie Harary, who have been the gateway for me to explore many of the ideas that are discussed, and works quoted, in this book.

I have spent more than the last decade in the Greater Washington, DC, area teaching Torah and personal growth to Jews from all walks of life, and so much of this book is an outgrowth of those teachings. Thank you to all of my students who have opened your hearts to learn from me, supported me, and have joined me on this journey to fulfill my dreams. I would especially like to say thank you to my wonderful partners and supporters in building the Lev Experience and for your excitement and encouragement about all of our projects, especially this one.

The staff of Mosaica Press are beyond wonderful. To Rabbi Doron Kornbluth, my deepest appreciation for your encouragement and your positivity from the first time we spoke, for your patience with me, and for helping me reimagine what this book can be.

I have been blessed with so many amazing family and friends who were excited to financially support this project. I cannot thank you enough. This project could not have happened without you.

Lastly, to my very special family. To my wife, Devorah, you are my partner in life, in work, and in this book. The world could have been collapsing while I was writing (sometimes it actually felt like it was), and I would have had no idea because by the time I emerged, you would have put it all back together. Thank you for your encouragement and excitement about this project and all of our projects together. And to my six beautiful children, thank you guys for being my biggest cheerleaders. Once you found out that I was working on a book, I knew there was no turning back!

While I have done my absolute best to offer an approach that is based on authentic Torah sources, it should be noted that while quoting sources out of their original context, I might have inadvertently misrepresented what the original authors' true intentions were. If that is the case, I accept full responsibility. Any misinformation should not reflect negatively on any of the authors quoted.

I pray that I have done my job well and have fulfilled my role in writing this book—as a "water-carrier"—by drawing from the teachings that have impacted my life and have shaped the way I approach the world. My intention and aspiration have been to deliver it to you, dear readers, in the clearest and most inspiring way that I could.

I welcome any feedback and comments and certainly any success stories that may result from reading this book. I can be reached at my email, shlomo@levx.org.

Shlomo Buxbaum
Silver Spring, Maryland
January 2021

INTRODUCTION
WHAT IS YOUR LIFE MISSION?

The day that you were born is the day
that God decided that the world
can't go on without you.

Chassidic saying

JEWISH TRADITION TEACHES that every one of us is put in this world with a specific mission that we must accomplish in our lifetimes. In a world of over seven billion people, you are unique. Just as no two people look exactly the same (even those identical twins whom you can never tell apart), no two people have the exact same personalities, strengths, or struggles. Neither you nor I are like anyone else who ever walked the planet! And it is our responsibility to express our uniqueness through our specific missions.

It is this beautiful diversity that allows humanity to thrive, as the full spectrum of human beings fill the different roles that are necessary to keep the world functioning. It also keeps human relationships dynamic, as different personalities come together to balance each other, challenge each other, and fuse together into a new, more improved whole.

Science may suggest that our uniqueness is nothing more than the molding of the variety of our life experiences. But it seems that our differences are rooted much deeper into our wiring, becoming apparent even at an incredibly young age. There are aspects of a human being's temperament that can be detected even within the first few days of life!

According to Kabbalah, the reason that no two people are similar from the day that man was created and onward is because every single person exists for a specific purpose; a predetermined, Divinely ordained mission that we are here to accomplish. We are each a piece of a massive puzzle, and without us, the world cannot be complete.

EVERY SINGLE PERSON EXISTS FOR A SPECIFIC PURPOSE; A PREDETERMINED, DIVINELY ORDAINED MISSION THAT WE ARE HERE TO ACCOMPLISH.

But do we ever truly know what that mission is? Can we discover it, and can we ever be certain that we are accomplishing it?

The secret to discovering one's mission in life was first taught to me by my grandfather, of blessed memory. He had escaped Germany in his younger years and was, by nature, a man on a mission. He was focused and serious. Every word that came out of his mouth was calculated, every action was intentional, and if you wanted to get a smile out of him, you would need to make a very compelling argument why. He wore a tie whenever he left the house and, to this day, I would not be surprised if he slept with it as well. I was his only son's only son, and, as the one carrying on the family name, it was important to me to live up to the high expectations that he placed upon me.

At the time that he taught me this essential lesson, I was a yeshiva student in Israel, full of plans and dreams of how I was going to "change the world"! I had begun dabbling in teaching and outreach, and, after having a powerful experience as mentor for a group of visiting college students who were in Israel on a Jewish learning trip, I was sure that I had discovered my mission.

I loved the philosophical debate, the deep conversations, and the opportunity to meet such a wide variety of people whose backgrounds were so different than mine. I relished the thrill of getting up in front of a crowd and sharing inspirational words and seeing the faces of the audience become enlightened. I cherished the experience of leading young Jews in song, strumming the few guitar chords that I was familiar with (that seemed to be the basis of every Jewish folk song), feeling the powerful emotions of the slow melodies and the adrenaline rush of the livelier tunes when the participants would break out in clapping or dancing.

During my time in Israel, I would correspond with my grandfather through good-old-fashioned written letters, and while I was generally excited to share with him my progress, I was even more enthused this time to tell him that I had figured out my life mission and to unveil my plan to change the world.

His response will stick with me until this very day:

> Dear Shloimeh [which is how he pronounced my name—with a thick German accent],
>
> While it is certainly a very good thing to change the world, remember that the real reason that you are placed in this world is to change yourself.

He then proceeded to unveil *his* plan as to how I—and every human being—must dig deep inside themselves for true self-discovery and go about reaching a very high level of self-mastery to truly fulfill what we have been placed in this world to do.

It is now almost twenty years later, and I did, indeed, pursue my passion. In my Rabbinic career, I have the opportunity to teach and inspire in many different roles and settings, and I still dream about how to "change the world." But more and more do I recognize the truth of the words of my grandfather—that our mission in this lifetime is more than just about "doing," it is about "becoming."

This is a book about living an empowered life by discovering and accomplishing your unique mission that only you can accomplish in this lifetime. A mission that begins by looking inward and becoming the person we can and need to become to accomplish that mission.

THE NEED TO DISCOVER YOUR MISSION

In a world where we sometimes feel so small and irrelevant, what can be more empowering than the realization that every single one of us matters tremendously—that every individual has something to contribute that no one else can! The great challenge, then, becomes the process of discovering and internalizing what it is that I am here to do. That is the first step to living a life of greatness.

Think about how so many successful people, great leaders, thriving companies, and organizations that are shaping the world spend so much time, effort, and resources crafting mission statements to clearly articulate the reason that they exist and what they hope to accomplish. It guides them in every decision they make and generates commitment and buy-in from employees and team members. As one great leader put it, "a company where the employees don't know the mission is like a soccer team that doesn't know which goal is theirs."[1]

Just as businesses thrive when they identify their mission, the same is true in life. Our mission is the guiding principle of our entire life, and when we identify it, all the various pieces begin to fall into place. We recognize what we need to do and why we need to be doing it, and we become more motivated to reach our goals. We gain a new understanding of our potential and a realization of the inner greatness that lives inside every single one of us. It feels as if we are making our mark—that every struggle matters, and that we are leaving our fingerprints on the universe in a way that nobody else could. It infuses every day of life with inspiration and passion. And during difficult times, it gives us an endless source of energy to draw from—one that cannot be extinguished no matter what life throws in our direction.

It is therefore worth whatever time and effort required to clarify what our mission is. That clarity could be the difference between living a life of fulfillment or one of emptiness. A life of joy or a life of sadness. A life of greatness or a life of mediocrity.

Often, when we contemplate our mission in this world, our minds trick us into believing that the answer is "elsewhere." We start to question our life circumstances and past decisions. *Had I only done this or been there!* Not to mention that we live in a social-media-driven world where we have constant exposure to others who seem to be making

---

1   Steven Covey, *The 8ᵗʰ Habit*.

a wide-reaching impact and look completely fulfilled. We are bombarded with everyone's successes and the most glamorous moments of everyone else's "perfect life": this one is crushing it in business, that one has created a massive following, this one is traveling the world, that one is looking really fit. It is natural to start to compare ourselves to them, wondering what we are missing out on and how we are doing in the eyes of everyone else. We wrongly assume that "they" are the ones accomplishing their mission because everything in their world seems so perfect. But what about lil' old me?

THE FIRST STEP ON THE JOURNEY TO AN EMPOWERED LIFE IS TO REALIZE THAT WE NEED TO LOOK NO FURTHER THAN THE LIFE THAT WE ARE ALREADY LIVING AND THE GIFTS THAT WE HAVE BEEN GIVEN TO ACCOMPLISH OUR MISSION.

The first step on the journey to an empowered life is to realize that we need to look no further than the life that we are already living and the gifts that we have been given to accomplish our mission. When we internalize this point, we let go of the frustration of trying to "fit in" and "keep up." All the comparisons fall away. We start to view ourselves differently, paying much closer attention to the things that make us different and taking pride in them. We realize that everything about us all contributes to our purpose. We embrace ourselves fully, feeling completely free to be ourselves and to express ourselves.

WHY I WROTE THIS BOOK

For over a decade, in my involvement in Jewish communal work as a rabbi, teacher, and spiritual coach, I have had countless personal conversations with individuals of all ages—from teens to young adults, to established adults with families and careers—and find that so much of what is on people's minds comes down to one major theme: Is my life today the life that I am ultimately meant to lead? In other words, *am I accomplishing my mission?*

That is not always the starting point of their question. They might present it as a spiritual struggle, dissatisfaction with their career or marriage, or a general feeling of sadness, burnout, or that something in their life is missing. But at the core, it comes down to a lack of understanding, or a misunderstanding, about what their mission is in this world.

And while the topic of finding one's mission has been written about and discussed at length both in the world of Jewish growth as well as in the general world of psychology and personal transformation, I have found that by and large, most of these discussions give focus primarily to pursuing one's strengths and passions, and not enough on the important inner work that is the real heart of why we are here.

SO MUCH OF WHAT IS ON PEOPLE'S MINDS COMES DOWN TO ONE MAJOR THEME: IS MY LIFE TODAY THE LIFE THAT I AM ULTIMATELY MEANT TO LEAD?

To be sure, strengths and passions are extremely important, and will be discussed in detail in this book, but our mission is much bigger than that. When we think about the wide range of experiences that we have in this lifetime, including all the joys and the pain, and the highs and the lows, certainly we would come to the conclusion that there is much more to our lives than just chasing the things that we are good at.

In this book, we will explore together how to view many different aspects of life through the lens of accomplishing your mission. My goal is to offer an authentic, Torah-based approach that I believe will put one's entire life in perspective as it has done for me. This work aims to show that everything in one's life contributes to that mission, and it cannot be accomplished by just emphasizing one or two aspects.

Additionally, we will explore very practical life tools and methods on how to go about achieving that mission. It is in this area that I have blended teachings that come directly from Jewish sources with many of the great tools that are being shared by the top thought leaders and high performers. In my own life, I have always felt that the wisdom of Judaism has taught me so much about life, and life has also taught me about how to live better Jewishly. There is more knowledge and wisdom at our fingertips than ever before in history, and much of it can help us gain new understandings and perspectives about how to become the best version of ourselves.

Finally, I have observed how so many individuals sadly believe that Judaism is nothing more than uninspiring trips to the synagogue, irrelevant Bible stories, ancient rituals, restrictions, and dogma. But this cannot be true! The heritage that spread the belief in the Oneness of God, that taught mankind that we are all created in the image of God, that inspired humanity to adopt the importance of loving your neighbor and showing kindness to all of creation, that has kept our people alive and thriving for thousands of years, despite our wanderings and persecutions, can't be that superficial!

The Jewish wisdom that inspired me in my life carries the secret to the more meaningful, vibrant life that every human being is looking for. It is full of daily practices that can provide us with exactly what we need to make us happier, more inspired, more fulfilled, and more successful at life. It carves out for us a lifestyle where we will see improvements in all our relationships and help us achieve more.

It is my ultimate goal for the reader to be exposed to Jewish teachings that will open up this door for them and inspire them to see the world through this light, to embrace these teachings and use them to discover and to accomplish their mission.

So, let us begin this journey together to discover our purpose and our mission and become the individuals that we were put in this world to be!

1

LIVING IN
TWO WORLDS

In the place that one's thoughts are,
that is where they exist.

Baal Shem Tov

IT'S A SMALL WORLD AFTER ALL

According to the laws of physics, one cannot be in two places at once. As young children, we usually learn this important fact of life as soon as we are old enough to ask a parent for help gluing our arts and crafts project while they are trying to get work done or prepare dinner for the family. This elicits the age-old response, "Do you think that I can be in two places at once?!" (That is about the same time in our life that we learn what rhetorical questions are.)

Metaphysically, though, we actually exist in multiple places at once. Firstly, we all exist in both an external world and in an internal world. Our external world is filled with the people whom we interact with, places where we go, and the environment that we are surrounded by. Our internal world is the world of our consciousness.

In this inner world, we are further fragmented by the various forces that exist inside of us that make us who we are: our character traits, emotions, thoughts, aspirations, and our spirituality. And at the core of our inner world is a spark of Godliness, the root of our souls, waiting to be nurtured into a full inner flame. In Kabbalistic literature, the external world is referred to as the *Olam Gadol*, the big world, while the human being is called the *Olam Kattan*, the small world, because of all of the various realms that exist inside of us.[1]

Across the Jewish world, a common value that is emphasized is that of *tikkun olam*, which literally means "repairing the world." This value is a central theme in Jewish life, mentioned in the daily prayer service that discusses a better future when "the world will be repaired with the Almighty's sovereignty."[2]

Tikkun olam is commonly used to refer to our obligation and responsibility to act kindly and try to make the world (the *Olam Gadol*) a better place. We often hear this term used in our Jewish communities in relation to charities, volunteer organizations, social justice initiatives, kindness projects, and other great causes that are working to improve the world. The term evokes the image of people taking care of the needy or fighting for civil rights.

The concept of *tikkun olam* is one of the most discussed points in Kabbalistic literature, not merely as a Jewish value, but as the very purpose for all of existence, the collective mission of humanity as a whole.[3] But the actual meaning of the term takes on a slightly different understanding. There, *tikkun olam* doesn't just refer to repairing the *Olam Gadol*, the big world, it refers to the repairing of the *Olam Kattan,* our inner world, as well. According to Kabbalistic tradition, every action that we do, every word that we speak, and even every thought is either elevating or damaging both our inner world as well as the world at large.

Tikkun olam, according to Kabbalah, isn't just about building organizations, fighting for causes, and posting hashtags; it is the mission of every single one of us through our day-to-day activities in both public and private, interpersonal and personal. The "big world" is only as

---

1   See *Malbim* in his essay called *Rimzei HaMishkan* on *Parashas Terumah*.

2   This line is said in the prayer *Aleinu*, which is said after each of the prayers.

3   See *Pesach Einayim* by the Chida, quoting the Arizal.

perfect as the sum total of all of the "small worlds" that make it up. And because we are each given a one-of-a-kind inner world that can only be refined through our own positive decisions and personal victories in the unique circumstances of our life, we find that we are each constantly engaging in *Tikkun Olam* in a way that only we can. Our inner world is one piece of a much bigger puzzle that only we can elevate.

As was said by the great fifteenth-century Kabbalist, Rabbi Isaac Luria, known as the Ari ("the Lion"), "No two people are similar from the day that man was created and onward, and one person cannot fix what is the responsibility for another to fix."

Because we exist in these two worlds, the external and the internal, our *tikkun*, our individual mission in this world, can also be described as two separate journeys:

- **The Outward Journey**—On the one hand, we are here to impact, to build, and to create. In a world that seems to be severely flawed, we are each placed here to fix it in any way that we can. To do this, we need to step up, self-actualize, and contribute. Regarding this aspect of our mission, we are expected to make a difference in the world, leaving behind a better world than the one we found when we got here.

- **The Inner Journey**—On the other hand, life is a journey inward, trying to go deeper and deeper to get to know ourselves better as we search for that deepest point, that spark of Godliness inside of us that never fades. Like a precious diamond hidden deep in the earth covered in dirt and minerals, we want to refine our inner world so it can truly shine with its full radiance and brilliance. It is through achieving self-mastery and greater awareness of our deepest self that we can accomplish this aspect of our mission. This second aspect of *tikkun olam* is also referred to as *tikkun ha'nefesh*, perfecting our inner world.

The two journeys will often overlap. This is because we can't truly impact the world in the way we are meant to without first becoming the people we were created to be. Like one great sage said, "Originally I dreamt of changing the whole world. I then realized that I should first try to change my community. I ultimately realized that if I want to change anything, I will need to change myself first."[4] It is equally as difficult to fully explore our inner depths without the experiences that come with trying to build the world around us.

WE CAN'T TRULY IMPACT THE WORLD IN THE WAY WE ARE MEANT TO WITHOUT FIRST BECOMING THE PEOPLE WE WERE CREATED TO BE.

Doing acts of kindness for others is a perfect example of this. It involves both the inner work of loving other people, suspending judgment, and detaching from one's possessions (be it money or time), but also the external work of seeking out opportunities and actually performing acts of kindness to others. Many people might be kind in theory, but weeks might go by before they actually do any act of kindness. Others might be performing acts of kindness externally, but carry inside them deep resentment or disdain for others, even the people they are showing kindness toward.

I once asked a group during a workshop on this topic to raise their hands if they viewed themselves as kind and selfless people. They all raised their hands. I then asked them what some of the common selfless acts are that they do on a day-to-day basis. The group was silent. I asked if anyone could share with me a selfless act that they did over the past month, and again there was silence. When I looked around the room, the looks on their faces told me that they were very surprised by the fact that they couldn't think of examples. Here they viewed themselves as selfless people, but could not actually find any examples to show that they were. At their 100th birthday party, there would be nothing to say about their kindness more than "they were selfless in theory." In this way, we see that the two journeys in many ways go hand-in-hand.

But despite this overlap, the focus of the journeys is very different. The external journey is about the impact that we have made and what we have tangibly accomplished. The inner journey is about the self-awareness, character development, and spiritual connection that was

---

4   Rabbi Yisrael Salanter.

achieved. The external journey is more about what we do; the inner journey is more about who we have become.

Therefore, even when it comes to acts of kindness, we will have two goals:

- The first is what we have externally *accomplished* through our kind act.
- The second is about what we have *become* because we did that act of kindness.

It is well known that the great Torah scholar and physician Maimonides advised that it is more powerful to do many acts of small kindness than to do one major act of kindness.[5] This is because when doing many small acts, it conditions one to become kind, more than doing one big act of selflessness. One might even make the argument that the greater beneficiary of the act of kindness isn't the recipient but the one who gave, because it gave him the opportunity to grow![6]

The inner journey, however, goes far beyond its application to the external world. It also involves us viewing ourselves as bigger than anything that we could accomplish in the physical realm. We are more than our relationships and more than our "doing." It involves us discovering our inherent self-worth. It involves tuning into a higher and more expanded level of consciousness where we meet the more Godly parts of ourselves.

THE "POINT" OF YOU

When I began teaching workshops on how to discover your life mission, I called it: *How to Discover the Unique "Point" of You.* When you hear the phrase "*point* of you," you probably think of purpose, an appropriate title for a class on discovering your purpose. But *point* also refers to the highest extremity of something, like the point of the pencil.

---

5   Maimonides, Commentary to *Avos* 3:15: "If a person gives 1,000 coins at one time and to one person, this is inferior to the one who gives 1,000 times with 1,000 coins...for the latter case multiplies the spirit of generosity 1,000 times over, while giving just once will awaken the spirit of generosity once, and then it ends."
6   See Talmud, *Bava Basra* 10a and *The Way of God* (*Derech Hashem*) 2:3, which explain that the entire reason that wealth and poverty exist is so that we can develop our character traits.

There is an old Jewish phrase that refers to a little inextinguishable spark of Godliness inside all of us. It is referred to in Yiddish as "*a pintele Yid*." *Pintele* (PIN-teh-leh) means "a little point," and *Yid* is translated as "Jew," a shortened version of the word Yehudi. *Yid* is also a variant pronunciation of the Hebrew letter *yud*, the tenth and smallest letter of the Hebrew alphabet. It looks like this: י. It is just a little dot, a little point or *pintele*. This little *pintele Yud* is the first letter in God's name, and therefore represents the point of Godliness inside of us. It begins as something very small, buried deep inside of us, but throughout our life our goal is to nurture it into a full inner flame. When you observe a person overcoming a great personal challenge or persevering in the face of spiritual adversity, you might comment, "That's the *pintele Yid* inside of him!"

So, as I like to say, *the point (purpose) of you is to discover the Point (Godly spark) of you.*

Your entire existence is about discovering that little point of Godliness inside of you. As we explore our inner world, as we discover our individual purpose, we also discover the tremendous depth that we have. If we go through life and never see that, we are missing out on one of the essential reasons that we are put in this world.

The goal of this book is to explore those two different aspects of our life's journey, as well as the many details that fall within them. We will first explore the elements of our inner world and the work that we need to do in each of those realms in order to "show up" to the world as the best version of ourselves. We will show the many ways that all human beings are similar, and where we each branch off to develop our own individual personalities. We will then learn how to embrace that individuality and map out a tailor-made strategic plan to live a truly empowered life that fully maximizes our specific strengths and navigates through our weaknesses.

Throughout this work we will be exploring the Torah roots of all of these ideas, specifically the Book of Genesis[7] and the stories of the Patriarchs and Matriarchs. There is a reason those stories were recorded

---

7   This is the Book of *Bereishis*, the first of the five books of the Torah. It begins with the story of the creation of the word and tells the stories of the Patriarchs and Matriarchs.

in the Torah for eternity and why they are written in the beginning as the foundation for all of the Torah. Beneath the story of our ancestors, there is a much deeper story. Your story. Your inner world, your external journey, your adventures, and your struggles all unfold in the early pages of the Torah.

Before we begin to define our mission, though, we must first take a deeper look at the whole concept of mission and what that means. Above, we spoke about how Kabbalah teaches that we are on a collective mission of *tikkun olam*, repairing the world,

BENEATH THE STORY OF OUR ANCESTORS, THERE IS A MUCH DEEPER STORY. YOUR STORY.

and how each of us has a piece of that mission that is designated to us. But what does this really mean? Is the world broken in some way that we need to fix it? And since we believe in an Almighty God, is fixing the world really our job or should we leave it to the One in charge?

As we said in the introduction, an employee cannot be fully motivated in their job if they do not fully grasp the mission of the company and understand what they are contributing toward! The more that the team knows their purpose, the more likely that they will be bought-in and inspired by the process. The more that we can see the full picture, the more we can understand how we fit into that picture.

So, let's begin our journey together by trying to understand what is the void that we are trying to fill and what is the end game that we are trying to achieve.

summary

In this chapter, we gave an overview of the purpose of man in this world. We showed that the well-known mission of *tikkun olam*, repairing the world, has two different aspects:

1. The "Outward Journey" to improve the *Olam Gadol*, the world around us, through our accomplishments and by making our impact on the world using the innate strengths that we were given.
2. The "Inner Journey" to improve the *Olam Kattan*, the world inside of us, through self-mastery, inner exploration, and discovering the Godly spark (the *pintele Yid*) that is inside of us.

2
THE GREAT GIFT
OF IMPERFECTION

Beloved is man for he was created
in the image [of God].

Ethics of Our Fathers 3:14

LIGHT AND DARKNESS

The Torah is Judaism's ultimate guidebook for living life to its maximum potential. All of the brilliant ideas that have ever moved humanity are in it. On the surface, it can come across to some as "merely" an extensive list of "dos and don'ts," some exciting stories, and a big book of brain-teasers to see how many theories could be derived from a vague text.

In truth, every verse, every story, and every law carry with them deep truths about our existence. Sometimes it's right there on the page; sometimes you have to scratch slightly beneath the surface; and sometimes you need to go way beneath the surface, but it is all there. Even the verses that seem to be irrelevant to our lives in the modern day contain lessons and values that can transform our lives. In fact, sometimes the verses that are the hardest to comprehend are that way because of the deep secrets that are hiding in them.

In the introduction, we showed how every successful organization rallies its constituents behind a carefully thought-out mission statement. To be most effective, the boss, coach, or leader aims to introduce that mission statement to his underlings as soon as possible—like on the first day of the job, if not earlier. So, we would expect to be introduced to the concept of our mission quite early in the Torah, and, indeed, that is the case! It's right there on "page one." Let's take a look together:

> *In the beginning of God's creating heaven and earth—the earth was complete emptiness, with darkness over the deep and God's spirit sweeping over the water—God said, "Let there be light"; and there was light. God saw that the light was good, and God separated the light from the darkness.*[1]

The light and darkness that exist on the first day of creation are somewhat mysterious. Can it be referring to the actual physical light that the eye can see? Let's keep in mind that the sun and the moon were only created later on the fourth day of creation. Surely, there is something deeper and more mystical being communicated to us.

We are all acquainted with using the terms "light" and "darkness" as symbolic of positivity and negativity. When we see someone do something good, we will say that they are shining their light onto the world. When someone is depressed, they will say that they are in a "dark place." Spiritual seekers search for "enlightenment," while the bad guys in movies come from the "dark side." Using light and darkness as a metaphor for good and bad is rooted in the Kabbalistic understanding of these first verses of the Torah.

Kabbalah teaches that the light of the first day of creation is what is referring to an *ohr ha'ganuz*, which means a hidden, Godly light. With the words "Let there be light," creation was being infused with the potential to be a place full of peace, joy, and harmony. A world where people truly love each other and selflessly give to one another, where people aren't in a constant state of inner struggle and

---

1 Genesis 1:1–4.

turmoil but live with serenity and authenticity. An "enlightened" world where we can sense and feel its spiritual essence and our own spiritual essence. The world that we all crave and dream about.[2]

So what happened?

> *God saw that the light was good, and God separated the light from the darkness.*

The commentaries explain that this great gift of an enlightened world was so wonderful and blissful, and *therefore* could not properly be enjoyed and experienced by any being who did not play an active role in building it.

Let's explore this idea.

As parents, my wife and I do this all the time. We have two types of gifts that we give to our children. There are the small gifts that we give as often as we can to keep our kids feeling joy, and to remind them that we love them and care about them and think about ways to make them happy. We don't ask them to earn it or to wait for it. They get it just because they exist.

And then there are the really special gifts. We have found that when we ask our children to earn it by improving their behavior or by trying to reach for a certain achievement, they feel so much more excited about these gifts and so much better about receiving them.

In our own lives, we see this all the time. We take great pleasure and joy from the achievements that we worked hard for or personal attributes that did not come easily. These give us so much more enjoyment in life than the things that came to us without any work. This clues us in to an essential truth about what it means to be a human being: we are hardwired inside to want to own our destiny and not be handed any freebies.

Because of this, we often find that people whose life circumstances forced them to work harder—either because they came from an underprivileged upbringing, or because they struggled with some sort of

---

2   See *Rashi*, Genesis 1:4.

disability—become happier and more confident adults if they have successfully overcome those challenges. This speaks to the greatness of the human spirit. Because we contain that Godly spark, as we mentioned above, we seek to emulate God, Who is strictly a Creator, not a consumer. We, too, look to create our life and the pleasure it gives us, and not just consume it.

WE ARE HARDWIRED INSIDE TO WANT TO OWN OUR DESTINY AND NOT BE HANDED ANY FREEBIES.

TIKKUN OLAM REDEFINED

It is because of this that God created a world with the potential to become enlightened but hid that light so that it would be earned. The Almighty purposely created a world that is imperfect in order to give us the opportunity to perfect it. By doing so, we become an active partner in building the world. Could God have created a perfect world? Of course! But what would be our role then? If everything was just handed to us, would we really find satisfaction out of life? If we were given a perfect world, we might have been able to receive a very basic enjoyment, but the true joy of a deep relationship that takes work, the joy of self-actualization, and the joy of meaning and purpose would be completely absent.[3]

So, instead, we were placed in a world that was less than perfect—or, more accurately, perfectly imperfect—a calculated effort to set the stage for us to enter and do our part by using the tools that we have been given to restore the world to its original potential.

Based on this, we come to understand that mankind is on a collective journey to take a world that the Almighty made intentionally imperfect and try to perfect it in order for us to become true partners in the building of this world. It is through this partnership with God that we access the hidden Divine light of creation. As we say in prayer three times a day, the ultimate vision of creation is when "the world will be repaired with the Almighty's kingship."

---

3   See *The Way of God*, sect. 1, by Rabbi Moshe Chaim Luzzatto.

This is the meaning of the verse in Psalms: "The heavens belong to God, but He gave the earth to mankind."[4] These incredible words bring out this idea. Though God never fully relinquishes control of the physical realm—constantly breathing life into it and guiding it toward its destiny—the actual road to get there is very much a partnership with humanity; our decisions and efforts determining how the trip will look. We therefore exist to maintain and improve the world that we were given and elevate it and bring it to its desired state.

In many ways, the entire story of humanity, one that continues to unfold, is all about rediscovering that hidden potential. All of the highs and lows of history are all part of this journey. THE ENTIRE STORY The collective mission of mankind is to navigate OF HUMANITY, ONE through those highs and lows until we learn how THAT CONTINUES to repair the world. And when we do, we become TO UNFOLD, active partners with God, showing what it means to IS ALL ABOUT be created in the "image of God." And every single REDISCOVERING one of us plays a role in that mission. THAT HIDDEN A core belief in Judaism is that we are always POTENTIAL. coming closer and closer to a time in the future when the world will be repaired. These days were spoken about throughout the Torah, and have been spoken about for generations through the words of our Sages and great rabbis. It is one of the fundamental tenets of Jewish belief, and it is woven into almost all of the prayer services. This promising vision has made such an imprint on human belief that many religions and spiritual traditions have some form of this dream as part of their tradition.

One could argue that if we take a look at history from a bird's-eye view, one could see that the general trajectory of humanity has moved in this direction. It seems that as each generation takes the stage, new movements, new advances, new technologies are paving the way for a new world. And while each generation discovers new challenges, all

---

4   Psalms 115:16.

of that seems to be part of the natural flow of high and low that comes with growing pains.

One can compare it to a successful company as it moves from a startup phase into a full-scale business. Many new problems may arise that might even threaten to destroy the company, but when the solution comes, the company gets propelled into even greater growth and further development. During the crisis, all hope seems lost, but in the grand scheme of things, one can see that this was just part of the process.

In our world, too, all of the pain is just part of the process, pushing us toward better days ahead. But until that time comes, there will always be pain in the world. We will see it globally through sickness and war; we will see it as a Jewish People through exile and anti-Semitism; and we will experience it personally in a variety of different ways. But problems lead to solutions, adversity builds muscle, and friction propels us forward so that through it all, we move closer and closer to a repaired world.

HOW YOU FIT INTO THE PICTURE

As we saw above, every single one of us is part of this process, though it is often difficult to see how. How does one's own personal growth process factor into what is certainly a gargantuan task of changing the world?

But it certainly does!

Kabbalah teaches us that the outer world (*Olam Gadol*) is a reflection of our inner world (*Olam Kattan*). As we grow as individuals, we are sending out positive vibrations to the world and adding more light simply by virtue of our improvement. And the more we grow, the more we will be able to impact the world around us with our positive energy in ways that we couldn't before. To quote once again those powerful words: "If I want to change anything, I will need to change myself first."

AS WE GROW AS INDIVIDUALS, WE ARE SENDING OUT POSITIVE VIBRATIONS TO THE WORLD AND ADDING MORE LIGHT SIMPLY BY VIRTUE OF OUR IMPROVEMENT.

This is true because there is a deep interconnectivity between all human beings. This is apparent on many levels. Think about how the coronavirus, COVID-19, spread from one individual to create a world pandemic. Though positive change doesn't work quite as fast, we can never underestimate the "butterfly effect" of our personal growth. As the old saying goes, "All boats rise with the tide." When you are growing, you are influencing the people around you in ways that you will never know. We are constantly inspiring people when we are growing in ways that we don't even realize, and those people carry the positive effect to others and them to others, etc.

This is the mystery of how great movements get started. An individual shares an idea with a small group of people, which starts a trend, which causes a snowball effect, with more and more people getting involved. At some point, the idea takes such firm root that it no longer needs to be taught. It becomes so deeply embedded in the psyche of humanity that it becomes a given. We are all constantly part of this process, either by being the originator of the idea or by being a chain in the process of spreading it.

We are spiritually connected as well. Modern psychology speaks about a "unified field of consciousness," where the inner states of all human beings are actually intertwined one with another.[5] So when one person is growing, the collective consciousness of society is becoming elevated. Judaism teaches that when a holy person enters a place, the entire city feels the presence, and when the holy person leaves, the collective spiritual connection of the place declines.[6] This means that we have the power to bring more light into the world simply by looking inward and becoming greater individuals.

This profound idea opens up the door for us to begin the journey of embracing our mission of *tikkun ha'nefesh*, perfecting our inner world. If we truly want to repair the world, we want to focus on repairing ourselves.

---

5   Judaism has a name for the spiritual interconnectivity of human beings. In Hebrew, it is called *arvus*. As in the term *"kol Yisrael areivim zeh la'zeh*—all of Israel are intertwined one with another."

6   See *Rashi's* commentary on Genesis 28:10.

But in order to repair ourselves, we have to ask the question: How well do we really know ourselves? Do we know who we are today? Do we know what we can be? Do we know why we act the way we act, and if we were to change ourselves, how would we go about doing so?

In our next chapter, we will take a deep inside look into ourselves to understand deeply how we operate and what our goals should be.

summary

In this chapter, we defined what it means to "repair the world" by showing the stages that the world has gone through and is still going through, including:

- the enlightened state that existed "in the beginning,"
- the concealment of that light so that mankind can become an active part of the creation process,
- mankind's constant struggle to improve the world throughout history and how all setbacks have led to further growth,
- the Jewish belief that there will be a time in the future when the world will return to its original state of enlightenment.

We showed how every single individual who comes into this world is playing a part in bringing the world closer to its enlightenment through all the work that we do in this world, including—and especially—the inner work that we do to improve ourselves.

3

CLIMBING THE LADDER OF OUR INNER WORLD

"He dreamt of a ladder set on the ground
and its top reached to the sky."

Genesis 28:12

THE FOUR ELEMENTS

Look deeply inward, and you will find a fascinating and complex inner world. We are all aware that man is a combination of a physical body and a spiritual soul. But, in fact, we are much more complex than that.

Judaism compares a human being to a ladder with its feet on the ground and its top reaching up to the heavens.[1] Each rung of the ladder represents a different plane of consciousness, a different realm that exists inside of us, each one loftier and more hidden than the one beneath it. We might naturally be more aware of the rungs on the lower part of the ladder, the ones that we experience in our everyday life in different ways, but as we develop ourselves, we gain greater awareness of the higher levels as well. This inner world is called in Hebrew our *nefesh*, which is commonly referred to as our "life force."

---

1   See *Alshich* on Genesis 28:12.

Because each one of these inner realms possesses its own character, needs, and drives, as we will see, it is not uncommon to feel turmoil inside of us, as if there are different personalities living inside of us. Within the same day, we can feel both completely content as well as dissatisfied with our life; we feel like we can conquer the world as well as completely helpless; we feel inspired and completely burned out, etc.

JUDAISM COMPARES A HUMAN BEING TO A LADDER WITH ITS FEET ON THE GROUND AND ITS TOP REACHING UP TO THE HEAVENS.

Our mission in this world is about ascending this ladder of consciousness by becoming a master over each realm, using it as a stepping-stone to reach even higher. Through this process, we will achieve a much more perfected and elevated version of ourselves. And if we are to really become masters of ourselves, we must understand how all these different faculties inside us operate and how we are supposed to bring inner harmony to all the parts of the machine.

If you want to fully comprehend the elements of any structure, you want to look closely at its blueprint. It follows then that if you want to understand the elements of your inner structure, you will want to delve into the blueprint of all of life, i.e., the Torah, and specifically the account of the creation of man. But one can only appreciate what happens at this moment of creation by looking at the steps leading up to it, i.e., the story of creation in its entirety.

WHEN THE TORAH TELLS THE STORY OF THE CREATION OF THE WORLD, WHAT WE ARE REALLY BEING TAUGHT ARE DEEP TRUTHS ABOUT THE BUILDING BLOCKS OF OUR INNER WORLD.

As we explained above, Kabbalah refers to the universe as *Olam Gadol*, the big world, while human beings are called *Olam Kattan*, the small world. This is because everything that exists in the external world on a macro level is reflected on a micro level inside us. This means that it will have some expression and manifestation in our inner world. (For example, just as the world goes through cycles of day and night, all human beings as well go through times of clarity and times of confusion.) In fact, Kabbalah would argue that the laws of science and physics are only like that *because* they reflect the same spiritual truths that can be found in our inner world.

Therefore, when the Torah tells a story of the creation of the world, what we are really being taught are deep truths about the building blocks of our inner world. The Torah is not meant to be a science or a history book, and certainly the story of creation does not serve any of those purposes. But if we delve into its deeper interpretation, we can develop an understanding of the inner map of human consciousness.

Let's take a look.

Just as the first step of creation—light—is speaking of a hidden spiritual light, as we explained, Kabbalah describes the entire story of creation along these lines—as an unfolding of sorts, where the completely formless hidden spiritual light of the first day takes on more and more form until the final step of creation, the creation of man.

The story of creation moves from the creation of light to the creation of a firmament (or sky) that "separates the waters" and then a gathering of the waters to expose land and vegetation. We see how all of creation for the first three days is an unfolding process:

- Day 1: Light that has almost no form and substance
- Day 2: A firmament made of gases, with slightly more form
- Day 2 and 3: Water, a liquid, with even more form and some density
- Day 3: Land, which has the most form and is completely dense

The cycle repeats itself in the second part of creation, days 4–6, with the inhabiting of each of those realms:

- Day 4—The sun and moon (related to light)
- Day 5—Birds (related to the sky)
- Day 5—Fish (related to water)
- Day 6—Land animals (related to land)

Based on this cycle, Kabbalah (and many other ancient philosophies) spoke of the four fundamental elements of creation: light/fire, air/

wind, water, and earth. These four elements reflect the four states that all matter exist in: Plasma, Gas, Liquid, and Solid.

ELEMENT	DAY OF CREATION	ACT OF CREATION
Fire	1 and 4	Light/luminaries
Wind/water	2 and 5	Sky and separation of waters / birds and fish
Earth	3 and 6	Vegetation / land animals

The final creation on the sixth day was man who, fitting the pattern, belongs on land. In fact, his physical body was metaphorically also created from the dirt: "Hashem Elokim formed man from the dust of the earth."[2] But what makes man unique in this story of creation is that while his physical body is associated with the lowest element, his inner world contains all the elements of creation that preceded him.

Based on this, when exploring the inner world of man, the various different domains that make up the *nefesh* can be said to follow the very same pattern. There will be parts of our *nefesh* that have properties that are light and formless like the element of fire, and parts of the *nefesh* that are heavy and dense like the element of earth, and those that are in between.

THE FOUR ELEMENTS OF OUR INNER WORLD

Though the Torah's story of creation begins with light and goes from formless to the densest, we will discuss the elements in the reverse order, beginning with the earth element and working our way "up." This is because, from the perspective of God's creation from nothingness to a world, it was a descent from completely spiritual to completely physical. Our life, though, is naturally directed in the other direction. Our consciousness and awareness are naturally more in tune to the more physical realms, and as we mature and become more refined, we become more in tune to the realms that are above that.

Let us see together how these four states of matter reflect our inner world. We will give an overview of what each level is, and in the

---

2   Genesis 2:7.

upcoming chapters we will go into greater detail about the various struggles that happen in each of these domains.

- Earth—the domain of the physical body
- Water—the domain of the emotions and desires
- Wind—the domain of the intellect and communication
- Fire—the domain of the will and self-awareness

EARTH: THE ELEMENT OF THE PHYSICAL BODY

The element of earth is the element that is connected to our physical bodies. At this level, our consciousness is most connected to our bodily needs, and our main drive is for survival and the basic needs that keep our body working and properly maintained, such as the need for food, shelter, safety, and reproduction. When we are tuned in to this plane of consciousness, the only active parts of our brain are those necessary to sustain our body and keep us alive. We focus on the world and its resources, and even other people, in terms of what they can provide for us.

This level corresponds to earth because just as earth has the most form and the least movement, this part of our consciousness craves security, stability and consistency, and it takes care of our physical body, which is the most dense part of the human being.

WATER: THE ELEMENT OF FEELINGS

Water is the element that corresponds to emotions and desires. At this level, we begin to see beyond just survival but look for ways to gain pleasure from this journey that we are on. It is here that we begin to experience sophisticated emotions such as love, fear, and hope, as well as lusts and cravings. Human interactions become less transactional, less self-centered, and more about companionship for emotional reasons.

The movement and life-giving power of water is symbolic of the pleasure and emotion that is found at this level. Just as water can be wild and rushing, our emotions can sometimes overwhelm us. However, when we are experiencing healthy emotions, they are like calm waters. The same is true with our desire for pleasure. Sometimes our cravings are raging and intense like the crashing waves, and sometimes they are very subtle like a lake at low tide.

We often associate our emotions and pleasure with our "heart" because just as the heart pumps oxygen and life throughout the body, our feelings provide us with the vitality to go about our life. It is the pleasure and pain felt at this level that inspires much of our actions.

WIND: THE ELEMENT OF THE INTELLECT AND COMMUNICATION

Wind is the element connected to our intellect and our ability to communicate. It is here that we seek wisdom, knowledge, understanding, and information to develop the perspectives and direction for our lives. It is driven not by pleasure and emotion but by logic and sensibility. Feelings are replaced with cognition. Ideas, intuition, and creativity are born. At this level, human relationships center around shared visions and common beliefs, and it is here that our feelings and thoughts are concretized to the point that we can process, articulate, and communicate.

Just like there can be a rapid wind or a calm wind, here, too, there are sublevels where thoughts can be scattered, wild, and distracting, or they can be calm and blissful. When the winds are rapid, we tend to talk a lot, but when the winds are calm, we experience less need to talk or feel the need to say only what is necessary.

The thinking/communication level corresponds to wind, which has almost no form and is intangible, just like one's thoughts. The wind also guides the other elements in the same way that the thoughts of a person guide him. It is wind that formulates breath for communication.

FIRE: THE ELEMENT OF WILLPOWER AND SELF-AWARENESS

Fire is the spiritual element connected to willpower, self-esteem, and motivation. It is here that our consciousness goes beyond the faculties that are most easily observed and enters into a domain that lies behind many of the decisions that we make and what guides us through life. It is here that our yearning for self-actualization and even greatness is rooted. At this level, we want to feel like we really matter. Feelings and thoughts are replaced with an inner yearning and drive. In our relationships, we feel a responsibility for others as if they are an extension of ourselves.

This level corresponds to fire. The element of fire is the most form-less, just as the will is detected least from all the other levels. Just like fire rises up, this level is about that inner yearning to go higher and higher. And just as fire destroys, this is the part of our self that we are tapping into when we are trying to overcome obstacles or remove any-thing blocking us from our path forward.

The four elements and their relationship to the four parts of our *nefesh* can also be visualized using the following model. The Earth Element is on the bottom and is the widest because it has the most form and density. As we ascend, it gets thinner, creating a triangle (sim-ilar to the famous Maslow's Hierarchy of Needs).

FIRE
willpower/
self-esteem

WIND
intellect/communication

WATER
emotions/pleasure

EARTH
physical/basic body needs

THE FIFTH ELEMENT

We have shown that there are four elements or states of existence in creation and four inner domains of our *nefesh* that correspond to these elements. However, it would be incorrect to say that we have reached the top of the ladder and that our inner world ends there.

What about our soul? We are all familiar with the idea that the essence of man is the soul. This is referred to as the *Nefesh Elokis*, the Godly life-force. The soul is an eternal part of us that lives beyond our years in this world. When we experience our soul, we are experiencing the truest form of "I." When we speak about our body, our emotions, our thoughts, or our willpower, we don't truly identify with any of those things as "us" but rather entities that play a role in how we operate. The true "I" is at the soul level. Our body, our emotions, our thoughts, and our self-esteem will change, but we will still be us. That is the highest level.

Where does it reside? On the one hand, the soul can be viewed as a so-called fifth element, one that is even higher and has less form than all of the ones that we previously mentioned.[3] In the great Kabbalist work, *Nefesh Hachaim*, the soul is described as follows:

> *Man is said to have been the "last" to be created because of his body, but he is also characterized as being the "first" to be created because his soul, which is the breath of God's mouth, is rooted in the highest spiritual world, which existed before creation even began.*[4]

As we will see later, however, the soul itself has different levels that parallel and permeate the other levels of our inner world so that when we experience our Godly souls, we are experiencing them through the garb of the other faculties. The great Kabbalist and philosopher Rabbi Moshe Chayim Luzzatto describes the soul as "having many parts that are bound to each other like links in a chain. Each of these are bound to the one below it until the lowest one is bound to the animal soul, which in turn is linked to the blood, and that is where the body and soul meet."[5]

THE STORY OF CREATION REVISITED

With this in mind, we now have a fascinating new appreciation for the story of creation and how it speaks directly to us! Just as the creation of the world begins in a formless state of pure light (connected to the element of fire) and then gains more and more form with the elements

---

3   See the commentary of the Vilna Gaon on Proverbs 22:5.

4   *Nefesh Hachaim* 1:5.

5   *The Way of God* 3:1.

that are established in the subsequent days, we also must view ourselves in that same way. At our highest level, we are light, we are fire, yearning to go higher and higher. We are then given an intellect and emotions to give that fire more form and a means to express itself. The final vessel that houses these elements is our physical body, connected to the element of earth, which will serve as the vehicle to carry out the tasks in the physical world.

And just as each realm becomes filled with various inhabitants, we, too, discover all sorts of movement and development on each of these planes of consciousness. The luminaries are shining down on the world just as the light of our will provides us with vision and direction. The birds and fish swarm the skies and the seas just as our endless stream of thoughts and emotions flood our intellect and emotions.[6] And the animals roam the land just as we are constantly pulled by physical and animalistic needs.

In the final step of creation, man is created with a body from the lowest elements but contains inside of him all of the other elements rising up until his spiritual soul that precedes the story of creation: "Hashem Elokim formed man from the dust of the earth. He blew into his nostrils the breath of life, and man became a living being."[7]

Additionally, he is given instructions:

"And God said, 'Let us make man in our image, after our likeness, and they shall rule over the fish of the sea and over the fowl of the heaven and over the animals and over all the earth and over all the creeping things that creep upon the earth.'"

These instructions can be understood in a deeper way. Rule over your thoughts, emotions, and physical desires by awakening the Divine image that is inside of you.

---

6   It is interesting to note that the water and wind elements seems to always be partners in the days of creation: firmament and waters on Day two; birds and fish on Day five. Perhaps this is because of the deep connectivity between our emotions and our intellect, which are really indivisible. Our decision-making process is heavily rooted in both of those domains.

7   Genesis 2:7.

USING EACH ELEMENT THE RIGHT WAY

Our mission in this lifetime is to reach a state of wholeness as a person, and in order to do this, it is necessary to make sure that we are whole in each of these areas. Not properly perfecting any one of these parts of ourselves will almost always manifest itself elsewhere, and proper attention to one area also sets the stage for growth in another area. Therefore, we must make sure that we are living a lifestyle that is physically healthy, bringing strength to the body, as well as bringing ourselves joy and pleasure, expanding our mind, self-actualizing, and growing spiritually.

Like any piece of complicated machinery, if one part of it is working great but another part isn't working at all—maybe it's even missing—the machine won't operate to its fullest capacity. We, too, need to fully explore and understand every part of ourselves to make sure that we are operating at full capacity.

With these four elements of our *nefesh* life-force, together with the *nefesh Elokis*, the Godly soul that we will speak about in more detail later on, we can fully understand the roots of our experiences, our character traits, and our inner struggles. In the upcoming chapters, we will explore how to strive toward perfection in each one of these areas, as well as the struggle that occurs on each of these levels. We will see that while we each have all of these aspects of our personality, there are certain ones that are more dominant than others. This can mean that we are stronger in some areas than others. It can also mean that we struggle in some areas more than others. As we begin to understand the different realms inside of us, we will also begin to understand where our personal development should be focused.

summary

In this chapter, we showed how the Torah's story of creation can be understood as the Torah's map of the inner world of man. This is because the four fundamental elements of creation each represent an aspect of our inner world:

- Earth—domain of the physical body
- Water—domain of the emotions and desires

- Wind—domain of the intellect and communication
- Fire—domain of the will and self-awareness

At the top of man's inner world is the *Nefesh Elokis*, the Godly soul, which has its own levels. The more that we gain self-awareness as to how our inner world works, the more that we will be able to perfect each level and come to a place of wholeness.

4

THE FOUR STRUGGLES TO ENLIGHTENMENT

The purpose of life is to correct
our character traits.

Vilna Gaon in his commentary on Proverbs 4:13

DEVEIKUS—HOW TO ATTAIN JEWISH ENLIGHTENMENT

There is one thing that all spiritual seekers have in common. It doesn't matter if they are from the east or from the west; whether they have beards or are hairless; whether they wear robes, turbans, or top hats.

The goal of all spiritual seekers is to achieve high levels of self-mastery so that rather than being controlled by emotions, desires, thoughts, and ego, the seeker becomes the master of them. When we reach higher levels of self-mastery, we eliminate much of the turmoil of life that comes from being controlled by our negative inner forces, and we can enjoy a much more joyful, peaceful, and blissful existence. As we gain more and more self-mastery, we can also begin to experience higher states of consciousness, including a greater awareness of one's self, of the Divine, and a deep sense of clarity and truth.

People from all walks of life have looked toward religion and many other movements or practices trying to attain this. They travel the world, invest money and time, and experiment with all sorts of different practices in their search to gain awareness of the higher parts of themselves. There are many different words in many different languages and cultures to refer to this, such as enlightenment, transcendence, bliss, samādhi, nirvana, and probably countless more.

WHEN WE REACH HIGHER LEVELS OF SELF-MASTERY, WE ELIMINATE MUCH OF THE TURMOIL OF LIFE THAT COMES FROM BEING CONTROLLED BY OUR NEGATIVE INNER FORCES.

Reaching this high level of consciousness and connection is indeed the focus of all of Judaism. It is referred to as *daas* (expanded consciousness) or *deveikus* (attachment). Throughout our life, we may in fact have experiences that give us a glimpse of these lofty levels, but it is only through climbing the ladder of self-mastery that we can really become deeply connected to this way of life and sustain it in everything we do.

The struggle for self-mastery requires us to refine our character traits and elevate them from their inherent imperfections. The ultimate goal is to reach these higher states and experience the pleasure and bliss that can be experienced in those states. By doing so, we elevate our soul and at the end of this lifetime return it in a more perfected state than when we received it.

In one of the seminal works on personal growth, called *The Path of the Just*, the author opens up the book with this idea, articulating it with these powerful and very famous words:

> Our Sages of blessed memory have taught us that man was created for the sole purpose of rejoicing in God and deriving pleasure from the splendor of His Presence, for this is true joy and the greatest pleasure that can be found.

In order to attain this level of enlightenment, however, we must first deal with struggles that happen in the domain of each of the four elements and become the masters over them. As we learn the behaviors and habits that awaken the positive aspects of these elements and eliminate the negative ones, we become more and more in tune to our *Nefesh Elokis*, which is our spiritual essence, our Godly soul. This awards us with the ability to live every moment with pure consciousness, a connection with the higher levels of our soul, and tangible experience of the Divine. Without self-mastery, our consciousness is locked into the lower levels of our *nefesh*, and our focus and our energy are spent in a constant state of struggle.

CHARACTER TRAITS AND THE FOUR ELEMENTS

The four elements are the roots of all our character traits, and therefore they are the foundation of our entire life. In Hebrew, our character traits are known as *middos*, which literally means "measurements." This is because all character traits that are rooted in the four elements can be channeled and expressed in either a positive way or negative way, depending how and when we use it. We refer to our character traits as "positive and negative," or "good *middos*" and "bad *middos*," only in relation to how they are expressed. In truth, human beings do not have parts of us that are inherently bad, but when our character traits are underdeveloped or mischanneled, they can certainly become corrupted.

When positively expressed, our *middos* bring us closer to others and help us perform at the highest level. When negatively expressed, our *middos* cause us to act inappropriately and to hurt our relationship with others as well as with God. When we refine these traits, we experience the full pleasure of this world and reach our potential. When we struggle with character flaws, we watch our worlds fall apart. For every negative trait, there is a positive trait that can counteract that and help us in our quest for mastery. Our ability to strengthen our good *middos* and extricate them from their negative counterparts—no matter how much it seems that they control us—is a major part of what is commonly referred to as "free will."

Understanding the four elements helps us in this process because the more we understand where the trait is rooted, the more we will understand the inner drive that is behind it and what we need to do to master it. In fact, the great Kabbalists explain that even though there are many different ways that our character struggles or bad *middos* manifest themselves in our lives, they are all actually rooted in four prime negative *middos*, each one connected to one of the four inner elements.[1] These are the four obstacles:

1. Sluggishness (which leads to laziness, sadness, depression, etc.)
2. Lust
3. Levity (wasting time/words)
4. Arrogance

They are connected to the four inner elements in the following way:

1. The Earth/Body level is the root of sluggishness and laziness, just as the earth itself is dense and lacks any movement. The heaviness of earth is also represented in the heaviness that we feel throughout our life when we feel stuck, not accomplishing anything, or just burned out. It is because the earth/body level is mainly concerned about survival that we feel anxious and concerned about the future, sometimes for no real reason at all. This contributes further to our sad and heavy state and also leads us to become jealous of others whom we perceive as having it better than we do.

2. The Water/Emotion level is the root of both an endless pursuit of pleasure, including pleasures and lusts that are forbidden, and unhealthy indulgences in things that are allowed. The movement and life-giving power of water represents our desire to experience the finer pleasures of life.

3. The Wind/Intellectual/Communication level becomes the root of levity, including wasting time and useless chatter when it is engaged in trivial matters. The blowing of the wind represents the constant flow of thoughts through our head, which can either be meaningful thoughts or silly thoughts. Wind also represents the breath that is contained in our words. A meaningful mind will produce meaningful speech. A frivolous mind will produce frivolous speech.

4. The Fire/Will level becomes the root of inflated ego and an endless desire to be shown honor and respect. Fire that rises to the

---

1   See *Shaarei Kedushah* 1:2; see also *Tanya* chap. 6.

top represents our desire for self-actualization and to matter. A person who becomes obsessed with their own self-worth will struggle with haughtiness and excessive pride.

Think for a moment about some of the negative traits that you may struggle with. Can you connect them to one of these four?

In the upcoming chapters, we will see how every single human has to struggle in some way with the four negative roots and to try to uproot themselves from these traits. The struggle does not look the same for any two people. Each one of these roots expresses itself differently in different people depending on the specific mission of that individual. Those who have mastered these obstacles experience their souls—not as a fleeting moment of awakening, but as a sustained, consistent level of consciousness (*deveikus*). Their bodies, emotions, thoughts, and wills are now vessels for the higher levels of their souls.

Before we delve into understanding these four struggles and how to achieve self-mastery, it is important to realize that the struggle with these four obstacles is so central to our mission in trying to discover our higher selves that it is actually the key to understanding the very first story of mankind, the story of Adam and Eve. With proper understanding of the events of the first day of creation, we will see how the purpose of the story of Adam and Eve is in fact to set the stage for the future mission of the entire human race.

A REALLY BAD DAY IN THE GARDEN OF EDEN

Let's go back to that Friday afternoon in the Garden of Eden as Adam strolls through Paradise with an unparalleled closeness to God.

It is important to realize that when Adam, the very first soulful human being, was created, he was in the most perfected and enlightened state of consciousness possible. Our Sages teach us that he "reached from the ground to the sky" and "from one end of the world to the other."[2] These words are meant to inform us about

---

more than just his impressive height; it is a reference to his inner world, of which he had complete mastery. When the Torah speaks of the Garden of Eden, the utopian home of the very first couple, we are referring not only to a very desirable piece of real estate. We are talking about a very desirable state of consciousness. Had the story of this very first couple turned out different, and had they remained in the Garden of Eden rather than being kicked out on the very first day of their existence, as we will see shortly, the state of humanity for all future generations would have been drastically different.

So, what happened?

Adam receives his first commandment not to eat from the Tree of Knowledge of Good and Bad, or he will die. We all know what comes next: The snake persuades Eve. Eve persuades Adam. And then the shame, the curses, and ultimately the eviction from the Garden of Eden. This eviction represents a lowering of their level of consciousness, a demise from their original enlightened state to a life of inner struggle and turmoil.

But let's take a close look at the language the Torah uses to describe the sin. When Eve first eats from the Tree we are told:

> And the serpent said to the woman, "You are not going to die, but God knows that as soon as you eat of it, your eyes will be opened, and you will be like Divine beings who know good and bad." When the woman saw that the tree was good for eating and a delight to the eyes, and that the tree was desirable as a source of wisdom, she took of its fruit and ate. She also gave some to her husband, and he ate.[3]

We see in this verse a very clear reference to the four elements that were previously mentioned:

1. The serpent appeals first to the woman's desire for self-actualization, connected to the element of fire by saying, "You will be Divine beings."

---

3   Genesis 3:6.

2. She then sees that the tree is "good for eating," a reference to the earth/body.
3. "A delight to the eyes" is a reference to the pleasure that is connected to the element of water.
4. "Source of wisdom" is a reference to the intellect, the element of wind.

The reference to the four elements in these verses teaches us exactly what this Tree of Knowledge of Good and Bad was all about. Up until they ate, Adam and Eve were so deeply connected to the high levels of their soul that they were almost completely unaware of the four elements that connect them to the physical world. The tree therefore lowered their consciousness so that they became much more connected to their lower selves and all of the struggles of the four elements that come along with it. This is why it is referred to as the Tree of Knowledge of Good and Bad. In other words, it is the tree of struggle.

So, what does their story have to do with you and me?

Kabbalah teaches us that every single one of our souls are connected to Adam and Eve, who represent the collective soul of mankind.[4] When they fell from their high level of consciousness, the collective soul of humanity fell from their exalted level. The story of humanity is the reparation of that very first day when Adam and Eve were evicted from the Garden of Eden. It would be the job of their descendants—and every one of our missions in this lifetime—to rediscover that original greatness by struggling with our own challenges of self-mastery.

THE STORY OF HUMANITY IS THE REPARATION OF THAT VERY FIRST DAY WHEN ADAM AND EVE WERE EVICTED FROM THE GARDEN OF EDEN.

As disappointing as the first story of humanity may seem, and as frustrating as it is for every single one of us to be in a constant state of internal struggle, there is actually another very important lesson in the story of Adam and Eve. This will not only provide us with a silver lining in the story but will also reiterate an important principle about our mission and purpose. Let us look a bit deeper into the story...

---

4   By Rabbi Yitzchak Luria, as recorded by Rabbi Chaim Vital, *Shaar Hagilgulim* 23:2.

FREE WILL—THE BEAUTY IN THE STRUGGLE

There is something puzzling about the entire story of Adam and Eve. What was the point of God creating a Tree that was not supposed to be eaten from? And why did Adam and Eve, fully enlightened beings, find it so hard to listen to the one commandment that was given to them?

Furthermore, listen to the very strange words of the instigator of the entire story—the primordial serpent, the Torah's "mascot" for desire and temptation who convinced Adam and Eve that it was actually a good idea to eat from the tree:

> *"You will not die, for God knows that on the day that you eat from it, your eyes will be opened, and you will be like Divine beings, knowing good and evil."*[5]

These words make almost no sense at all. How could lowering their consciousness and being connected to the struggle between good and evil that comes with being connected to the four elements be considered "opening your eyes"? And how does it make them "like Divine beings"? How could Adam and Eve have fallen for this?

To understand this, we need to remind ourselves of a principle that we discussed earlier. All imperfection in the world exists for the sole purpose of giving man the ability to become a partner in the creation process and discover the ultimate joy of achieving and owning his destiny. When we personally struggle to achieve enlightenment, as opposed to it being gifted to us for no reason, we experience an even greater delight.

Adam and Eve had a taste of bliss when they were in the Garden of Eden, but they understood that there was something missing. They knew that there was an even greater potential that they couldn't access in the Garden of Eden where everything was so perfect for them. They

---

5   Genesis 3:5.

understood that if they would be challenged, they would be able to reach an even higher state than before. Instead of remaining in a constant state of euphoria and bliss and living with a constant clarity and awareness of God in their life, the Tree of Knowledge was a ticket into a world where man is smack in the middle of a pull between what is good and bad. In essence, this was the Tree of free will. And it is free will that leads to even higher levels.

This was the serpent's convincing argument. If you eat from it, you will indeed lower yourself, but eventually you will fight through all the challenges and temptations and get back to this place of Eden—and be even greater than you were before. There was just one flaw in this logic. Adam and Eve were not yet strong enough to withstand those challenges. Had Adam and Eve waited longer and spent more time in their holy state, eventually they would have been spiritually strong enough to enter into the struggle and be victorious. But they were not there yet. The sin of Adam and Eve wasn't that they ate from the Tree. It was that they ate before they were ready.

As a result, it is now our mission to undertake that inner struggle and discover our own hidden potential. And when we do, we actually discover the most delightful state possible. Even though there are times in our life when we feel that our imperfections and shortcomings are beyond repair, it is crucial to realize that it is this struggle that is precisely why we were put in this world, and it is our ticket for greatness. As the great Chassidic master Rav Tzadok said: "In the areas that a person struggles and repeatedly falls, it is in those areas that he is destined for greatness."[6]

Self-mastery is a task that can certainly be accomplished. The story of humanity is one that features generation after generation of men and women who struggled and overcame; who found a path in their life of amazing spiritual growth and transformation; who have lived empowered lives of this true inner joy and bliss. They are not any different than me or you. These are not only people of the past. They don't live in

6   *Tzidkas Hatzaddik* §49.

faraway lands or as hermits in caves. They are modern-day human be-ings who wake up with a mission and spend their days improving themselves and the world around them. They might fall and fall again, but they get back up and keep on fighting. And they learn the secrets and the habits that are necessary to elevate the inner elements.

THE STORY OF HUMANITY IS ONE THAT FEATURES GENERATION AFTER GENERATION OF MEN AND WOMEN WHO WHO FOUND A PATH IN THEIR LIFE OF AMAZING SPIRITUAL GROWTH AND TRANSFORMATION.

In the upcoming chapters, we will explore these four areas of struggle in greater detail, as well as the secrets and habits necessary to reach self-mastery. In doing so, we will climb the ladder of our inner world and discover what it is like to experience true higher consciousness and true *deveikus*.

summary

In this chapter, we learned that *deveikus*, or Jewish enlightenment, can only come about by mastering our four inner elements and the *middos*, thereby perfecting our *middos*/character traits. We learn this from the story of Adam and Eve, who were lowered from their original enlightened state when they caused damage to the four elements by eating from the Tree of Good and Evil. The four primary negative *middos* are:

1. Sluggishness, connected to Earth;
2. Lust, connected to Water;
3. Levity (wasting time/words), connected to Wind;
4. Arrogance, connected to Fire.

5

THE FOUR STRUGGLES IN ACTION

*A river issues from Eden to water
the garden, and it then divides
and becomes four branches.*

Bereishis 2:10

THE WORLD GOES SOUR

History has been dramatically shaped by the four roots of character struggle. Wars have been fought, empires have crumbled, homes have been shattered, and lives have been lost. And the very cause of it all boils down to just the same issues that a struggling married couple, a confused teenager, or an adult going through a midlife crisis might be discussing with their therapist.

It is only those who have a great awareness and an understanding of the four struggles that are able to overcome it. The better you know your opponent, the more likely you are to emerge victorious. And the forces that oppose living a life of greatness are the four character struggles.

Therefore, the ultimate playbook for success in this lifetime, the Torah, has much to say on this topic.

The first book of the Torah, the Book of Genesis, is, in fact, completely dedicated to just that!

It is the foundational book of the Torah, containing very few actual commandments but is rich with the stories of our ancestors. Through those stories, it attempts to convey to us the foundations of all growth, upon which all the instruction found in the next four books are built. On a quick glance at the book, one sees no obvious pattern or central lesson. There seem to be many stories, all of them interesting, some more exciting than others, but they don't seem to be conveying any specific approach to self-growth...until you scratch a little beneath the surface.

Upon greater study, one can see that the entire book is actually one story with one central theme pulsing through it. The book of Genesis is indeed all about mastering the four inner realms that we have been discussing.

Let's look at this on a deeper level.

As we saw in the last chapter, the fall of Adam and Eve plunged human consciousness down to the lowest levels of the inner ladder, where we were now destined to struggle with the four roots of struggle. The Torah then goes on to discuss the "evolution" of mankind in a world steeped in these struggles. Early on in the book of Genesis, four stories will be highlighted to illustrate the demise of mankind. Ultimately, our Patriarchs and Matriarchs will arrive to change the trajectory of mankind.

The four stories are:

1. Adam and Eve's son, Cain, kills their other son, Abel, in a state of depression and jealousy;

2. God destroys an entire generation with a flood (with the exception of Noah and his family) because the generation is filled with immorality;

3. The world rebuilds, only to unite against God by trying to build a tower that will cut off their ties to heaven and allow them to live a life that they please without any repercussions;

4. Shortly later, we learn about two extremely affluent cities called Sodom and Gomorrah, which are infamous for their evil ways, specifically in how they treat those outside of their affluent communities.

Looking closely at these four different stories, we see both subtle hints and clear manifestation of the four obstacles to self-mastery.[1] The pattern looks like this:

ELEMENT	STRUGGLES	STORY
Earth/body	Sluggishness, sadness, jealousy	Cain and Abel
Water/emotion	Lusts, indulgence	Generation of the Great Flood
Wind/intellect	Levity, idle chatter	Tower of Babel
Fire/willpower	Ego, excessive pride	City of Sodom

Let's examine each of these four stories so we can understand more about each of the elements and how they lead to struggle.

STORY #1: CAIN, ABEL, AND THE EARTH ELEMENT

The two sons of Adam and Eve are Cain and Abel. Cain is a "worker **of the earth**." Abel is a shepherd. Both bring an offering to God, but since Cain is stingy with his, God only accepts Abel's. At this point, Cain experiences a whole series of emotions: he is jealous, depressed (in the language of the Torah, "His face was fallen"[2]), and angry. He quarrels with his brother and murders him. The earth is faithful to Cain and "swallows" Abel's corpse, and is later included in God's curse to Cain.[3]

We can immediately see the connection to the first obstacle. The earth element in a person represents the physical body, our survival instincts, and the need to feel secure. It is our survival instincts that are connected to our very base, primal concern that the world cannot provide for all of us. This means that no matter how much we have,

---

1   See *Aderes Eliyahu*, Exodus 9:14; *Nesivos Shalom, Ethics of Our Fathers*, chap. 4.
2   Genesis 4:6.
3   Ibid. v. 11.

there is always a voice inside of us that creates concern about what the future will bring and makes us feel insecure with who we are and what we have. This makes it harder for us to be present, enjoy the life that we have, and open our hand to give freely to others. And when we see someone else doing well, it creates a sense of jealousy, as if somehow, what *you* have is taking away from what *I* should have.

Additionally, the heavy dense nature of earth represents the part of us that often feels down and depressed. We feel like everyone else is moving past us in life and we are just stuck where we are. This causes us to further underachieve. Therefore, a natural outgrowth of being in a heavy, dark state is that we start looking at others with a jealousy and spite.

THE HEAVY DENSE NATURE OF EARTH REPRESENTS THE PART OF US THAT OFTEN FEELS DOWN AND DEPRESSED.

There are times in everyone's life where they feel inner sadness and low energy. It is a natural outgrowth of our inner earth element, a part of being human. The great Kabbalist and philosopher, Rabbi Moshe Chaim Luzzatto, writes in *The Path of the Just* about the tendency of the earth element inside of us to bring us down:

> *A person's natural tendency is to be very sluggish. This is so because the earthiness of physicality is dense. It therefore keeps a person from desiring exertion and labor. One who wishes, therefore, to attain the service of the Creator, may His Name be blessed, must strengthen himself against his nature and be zealous. If he leaves himself in the hands of his sluggish nature, there is no question that he will not succeed.*[4]

Looking back at our story, we can now understand what Cain, the worker of the earth, is teaching us. The very name Cain comes from the Hebrew word *kinah*, which means jealousy. He seems to embody every aspect of the corruption of the earth element. He is in fact a man of the earth, and shows us extreme constriction through his stinginess,

---

4   *The Path of the Just (Mesilas Yesharim),* chap 6.

sadness, and jealousy, to which God warns him by saying, "Why are you so sad? Step up and you will succeed!"

And, indeed, we find that Cain's punishment is related to earth:

> *Therefore, you shall be more cursed than the ground, which opened its mouth to receive your brother's blood from your hand. If you till the soil, it shall no longer yield its strength to you. You shall become a ceaseless wanderer on earth.*[5]

STORY #2: THE FLOOD AND THE ELEMENT OF WATER

Over the next ten generations, mankind descends into a state of complete moral depravity. Specifically, the world becomes filled with theft and forbidden desires. The Torah states, "The powerful people saw how beautiful the daughters of men were and took wives from among those that pleased them (even those that were forbidden to them)."[6] Eventually, God decides that mankind, with the exception of the righteous Noah and family, should be destroyed. God decides to destroy the world and specifically uses a flood of water to do so.

Here, too, the connection leaps off the page. The water element in a person represents their emotional/pleasure level. It is at this level that we experience both a positive yearning for love and connection, as well as the negative pull toward physical gratification. In fact, research has shown that both feelings of love as well as physical pleasures activate related areas in our brains, known as pleasure centers, in a section called the striatum.

The close relationship between the two shows us that desire for physical pleasure used correctly is a powerful tool that leads to love or to enhance existing love. This is why so much of our relationship development happens over food. We go out to eat on dates, bring our families together for dinner, and try to get to know people over coffee. This is also why physical intimacy is an incredibly powerful tool to fuse

---

5   Genesis 4:12.
6   Ibid. 6:2.

two people together—not just on a physical level, but on an emotional and even spiritual level as well.

Just as water is the source of all life and growth, it is the love and connection that we feel that is the source of all of our vitality. When we feel loved, we feel a great sense of pleasure. Just as our bodies are about sixty-percent water, our inner life force is powered by the spiritual element of water, the love and connection that we feel. Still, the reverse of this is also true. When we feel that we are lacking love and connection, we begin to feel a strong inner emptiness, and our brains look for an easy way to substitute the drought that is caused by our loneliness. We naturally gravitate toward substituting that desire for pleasure with other pleasurable experiences that give us a "quick fix," fooling our brains to temporarily think that everything is good. This can lead us to indulge in excess pleasure and generate feelings of lust and inappropriate desires.

JUST AS WATER IS THE SOURCE OF ALL LIFE AND GROWTH, IT IS THE LOVE AND CONNECTION THAT WE FEEL THAT IS THE SOURCE OF ALL OF OUR VITALITY.

It is for this reason that mental health professionals have found that many clients that have fallen into the trap of some addictions were really at their core looking for love and connection. The void in their hearts that really needed to be filled with love and affection now causes them to look to supplement that lack by indulging in other pleasures that would give them a false sense of satisfaction, such as food, sugar, alcohol, drugs, cigarettes, or pornography, etc.

Water only provides life and goodness when in the proper measure and when properly channeled. An overflow of water, however, can bring destruction and devastation to the world. This is true about physical pleasure as well. When we indulge in physical pleasure more and more with no boundaries at all, it turns into lust and obsession. It becomes a distraction, hurts our pride, and zaps our energy, and eventually it can turn into an unhealthy habit or addiction. The inner pure desire to feel love and connection is replaced with an unquenchable thirst for more physical pleasure. We care less and less about people and more and more about ourselves, and life begins to fall apart. It is because of this that we find that illicit physical pleasures are referred to in the Torah as "stolen waters."[7]

As human beings, we are constantly being challenged to choose between how we will use this power of water that resides inside of us. Because this energy is so strong, it can easily be taken advantage of by others, used against us to try to sell us products by luring us with temptations that will capture our attention for their own good. We are challenged to develop the inner strength to decide that that is not where we want to focus these energies but rather to channel them toward the more authentic reason why we are given them: to build powerful, deep, intimate connections.

The generation of the flood got caught in a world of indulgence, lusting after whatever their eyes saw, as is indicated in the verse: "the powerful people *saw* how beautiful the daughters of men were." This echoes the words the Torah uses when Eve looks at the forbidden fruit and sees that it was "lustful for the eyes." The struggle between lust and love manifests itself strongest in the eyes. Our eyes hold the secret to deep love, when two people look into each other's eyes and connect deeply. But the eyes can entrap us in all sorts of places that will arouse illicit pleasure, from inappropriate images to looking at someone else's belongings. It is no coincidence then that the eyes are the most "watery" part of us, and that our strongest emotions are expressed through the water in the form of the tears that flow from our eyes when we are feeling deep emotions.

It is because of this that God decided to destroy the generation that abused the power of water with a very fitting punishment—a flood of water.

STORY #3: THE TOWER OF BABEL AND THE ELEMENT OF WIND

We now fast-forward another ten generations. The Torah tells a very brief story about a generation that tried to rebel against God. It begins by letting us know that "the entire land was of one language and uniform

---

7   Proverbs 9:17.

words."[8] This commonality of their speech plays an important role in their downfall and seems to be the trigger of their deciding to "build ourselves a city and a tower with its top in the heavens, and [to] let us make ourselves a name,"[9] which is interpreted as some sort of act of rebellion against God.[10] God does not approve of this behavior and responds by declaring, "Let's confuse their language so that one will not understand the language of his companion." He then scatters them upon the earth. The immediate theme that jumps out at us is the perversion of speech.

The wind element in a person represents their intellect and is manifested through their words, the wind of their mouth. One who has not become a master of their wind element is not in control of their thoughts. They will become easily distracted from focusing on what is important and fill their heads with nonsense. This nonsense is then expressed in the topics of their conversations and their mannerisms of speech.

Mastery in this area requires immersing oneself in intellectual pursuits that deeply matter, such as gaining a deeper understanding of the world and humanity for the sake of making the world a better place. It involves developing one's brain to think clearly and ethically. And, at its highest level, it involves searching for truth and trying to understand the will of God.

ONE WHO HAS NOT BECOME A MASTER OF THEIR WIND ELEMENT IS NOT IN CONTROL OF THEIR THOUGHTS.

The development of one's intellect is manifested through their speech by concretizing the thoughts with clear articulation, as well as the dynamic sharing and debating of ideas and beliefs.

The generation of the Tower of Babel did just the opposite. It was a generation of brilliant architects who could have designed cities and technologies to build a beautiful world. Instead, they abused their intellectuality and their "uniformity of words" to rebel against God. The location was thereafter called Babylon, whose name is also the origin of the English word "babble," which means silly and irrelevant speech.

---

8   Genesis 11:1.
9   Ibid. v. 4.
10   Some understand that the actual tower that they were building would be used as a deity using mystical incantations, thereby completely corrupting their aspect of speech.

Their punishment, measure for measure, was that they should be scattered, a term that brings to mind the property of wind, which scatters things far and wide.

STORY #4: SODOM

The next major sin that is discussed in the Book of Genesis is the sin of Sodom. Sodom was a city of affluence and plenty, so much so that the Torah says that it was "well-watered...like the garden of God."[11] It was also an inhospitable city that exerted its strength and power to abuse their guests. The Torah refers to the sin of Sodom as heavy.[12] The word heavy in Hebrew, *kaveid*, has the same letters as the Hebrew word for pride, *kavod*. This is echoed by the great prophet Ezekiel:

> *Only this was the sin of your sister Sodom: arrogance! She and her daughters had plenty of bread and untroubled tranquility; yet she did not support the poor and the needy. In their haughtiness, they committed abomination before Me; and so I removed them, as you saw.*[13]

The fourth obstacle is pride and ego, and it is connected to the element of fire. The element of fire always rises up. It therefore represents passion and motivation and is meant to drive us to become authentically great. But it can also be abused when we use it to just become more powerful than other people. In that sense, the fire is being used to destroy. Our goal should be to become inherently great, but when our goals are just about becoming *better* than others, that is the corruption of the element of fire.

THE ELEMENT OF FIRE ALWAYS RISES UP. IT THEREFORE REPRESENTS PASSION AND MOTIVATION AND IS MEANT TO DRIVE US TO BECOME AUTHENTICALLY GREAT.

The pursuit of honor comes from the need for self-worth. An essential need of every human being is to feel like they matter. This is what drives us to try to accomplish more in this world

---

11   Genesis 13:10.

12   Ibid. 18:20.

13   Ezekiel 16:49.

and to earn the feeling of satisfaction that comes along with those accomplishments. As a child, we are built very much by the compliments that our parents and teachers give us, as well as the attention that we get from our friends. A child who is not getting enough of that positive feeling will act out or get in trouble because that too gives the inner feeling that he or she matters—if not in a positive way, then at least in a negative way. As the child matures and further looks for attention, this same struggle will exist. He or she is presented with many ways to authentically matter but also many ways to create an outer facade that will call attention to themselves and create a false sense of self.

Most people that we encounter who come across as full of themselves are typically displaying a protective fence behind some deeper sense of insecurity. The outer demonstration of self-worth is to create optics to divert people's attention away from what might be going on inside. When a person feels healthy self-esteem, they are able to drop that guard.

The people of Sodom allowed themselves to become haughty, though not because of any real accomplishment but rather because they lived in a beautiful land and had plenty. They measured themselves by what they had, i.e., by their externals. The shiny outside was glossing over a very weak and poor inside. Since the society of Sodom used fire the wrong way, it is no wonder, then, that they were destroyed with fire.

These four stories summarize the first epoch of mankind, which was filled with world corruption, and we now see how each story is connected to one of the four elements and the connected struggles. To summarize:

THE CULPRIT	THE FLAW	THE PUNISHMENT
Cain kills Abel	Jealousy/sadness	Cain must roam the earth; the Earth is cursed
Generation of the Flood	Powerful men looking to satiate their lusts	They are destroyed by water
Tower of Babel	Uniting against God using the power of words	Their speech becomes confused; they are scattered (like the wind)
City of Sodom	Wealth and arrogance; mistreatment of people not from their community	They are destroyed by fire

But then the pendulum swings. After these mistakes, the Torah then discusses the Patriarchs and Matriarchs, with each family perfecting another level. In the stories of our Patriarchs and Matriarchs, the Torah gives us tools to reclaim the four levels of our personality and achieve self-mastery. In the upcoming chapters, we will explore the traits of greatness that are necessary to overcome the four roots of struggle.

summary

In this chapter, we saw how the early stories of the Torah, the evolution of mankind after Adam and Eve, are all meant to show us the four struggles in action:

1. The story of Cain killing Abel is a story of sadness and jealousy connected to the element of earth.
2. The story of the Generation of the Flood is the story of lust and is connected to the element of water.
3. The story of the Tower of Babel is about corrupted thinking and speech, connected to the element of wind.
4. The story of the city of Sodom is about their arrogance and is connected to the element of fire.

The Torah will then go on and teach us about how to fix these four attributes through the stories of the Patriarchs and Matriarchs.

6

ROADMAP TO GREATNESS

*Be bold as a leopard, light as an eagle,
quick as a deer, and mighty as a lion to do
the will of your Father in Heaven.*

Ethics of Our Fathers 5:20

WERE YOU TO MEET someone who has achieved absolute self-mastery, true enlightenment, how would you describe him or her? What would be the attributes that would shine through?

At this point in our discussion, we know what obstacles they would have to overcome, so we know what they would *not* be:

- They would NOT walk around with a negative energy about them and would not display laziness or jealousy (the struggle of the earth element).
- They would NOT be lustful or indulgent (the struggle of the water element).
- They would NOT be found wasting their intellectual power and engaging in idle chatter (the struggle of the air element).
- They would NOT come across as arrogant or narcissistic (the struggle of the fire element).

This is helpful, but we did not come into the world to be full of "nots." Is our mission nothing more than a long not-to-do-and-not-to-be list?

To truly get excited about our mission, we want to paint a picture of what true greatness looks like—a portrait of a true master of character—and understand what the tools and tactics are that we can utilize to become that person. The more that we can visualize what that looks like—both the journey and the destination—the more that we are likely to follow that path and manifest that image in our own life.

In this section, we are going to take a deep dive into the traits that we are put on this world to acquire. In order to do so, we are going to look toward both the words of the Written Torah, the handbook for greatness, as well as the words of our Sages in the Talmud.

We are going to closely examine a model of greatness to help give direction as to what the attributes that we want to develop are, as well as the achievements we would like to accomplish in our time here on this earth.

OUR PATRIARCHS AND MATRIARCHS

Jewish tradition teaches that every single person should ask the question: "When will my attributes resemble the attribute of my ancestors?"[1] Additionally, Jewish tradition teaches that "all of the events that happened to our ancestors are symbolic to the experiences of their descendants."[2] This means that we are supposed to view the stories of our Patriarchs and Matriarchs not just as stories from the past but as timeless lessons from the ultimate role models. As the saying goes, "The more things change, the more they stay the same."

Furthermore, Kabbalah teaches that the Torah can be understood on many different levels. On the surface level, we are learning important stories about important people. On a much deeper level, these people are actually archetypes of attributes and experiences that exist inside of us, so we all have an inner Abraham and Sarah, Isaac and Rebecca, and

---

1   See *Tanna D'bei Eliyahu*, chap. 25.
2   *Midrash Tanchuma, Parashas Lech Lecha* 9.

so on. They embody different parts of ourselves, and therefore their story is always repeating itself in the inner world of our psyche.

With that in mind, we will walk along their path, follow their footprints, and pick up the most important tools that we can apply to our life to fulfill our very own mission in this world.

ON A MUCH DEEPER LEVEL, THE PATRIARCHS AND MATRIARCHS ARE ACTUALLY ARCHETYPES OF ATTRIBUTES AND EXPERIENCES THAT EXIST INSIDE OF US.

We will learn how to have boundless energy and joy, to channel our pleasure toward deep loving relationships, to become master thinkers and conversationalists, and to lead with humility, until we ultimately climb the ladder of our inner dimensions and experience the highest levels of our soul and *deveikus* (attachment with the Divine).

Before we go deep on this journey, let's take a bird's-eye view at the model of greatness that we will be discussing. See the overall model and how the pieces fit beautifully together. In the following chapters, we will look at each one of these in-depth.

NEFESH LEVEL/ ELEMENT	OBSTACLES	HOW TO ELEVATE	PERSONIFIED BY
Body level/ Earth	Sluggishness Laziness Sadness Jealousy	Energy Joy Consistency of habit Abundance mindset	Abraham and Sarah (Rebecca)
Feeling level/ Water	Lust	Channeled pleasure Deep love Hope	Isaac and Rebecca
Intellectual level/Wind	Wasting time False beliefs Idle chatter	Intellectual honesty Pursuit of truth Meaningful communication	Jacob Rachel and Leah
Will level/Fire	Inflated ego Pursuit of power Anger	Humble and fearless leadership	Joseph Judah King David

THE POST-GAME INTERVIEW

Before we begin on this journey down the path of our forefathers, it is important to examine a powerful idea from our Sages that will help guide us on our journey. In a powerful piece of Talmud, our Sages describe the Heavenly scene after we die when our souls are standing before the Heavenly tribunal seeking to enter into the paradise of the Next World. We are told by our Sages that there are actually seven achievements that we are asked about, and if we can answer in the affirmative, we will be able to consider our life a success.

Before we list the seven, it is important to realize that our Sages are actually tapping into a powerful tool that is still used today as a common practice to get one really thinking deeply about where one's life is going. Though it might seem that thinking about dying would be a very depressing way to use your imagination, it doesn't have to be. Many growth-oriented people have the practice of writing their own eulogy to really get clarity on what is important to accomplish while they still have the time left. This is one of the most powerful and motivating activities you can do. (In one practice in North Korea, you actually spend ten minutes in a coffin contemplating what you would like to write.)

The famous story of why Alfred Nobel invented the Nobel Peace prize proves the point. Nobel had invented many things—most notably dynamite, at the age of thirty-four. But despite his success, Nobel had a rude awakening about what he would be remembered for when the newspapers accidently published an obituary about him while he was still alive.

After his brother, Ludwig, died, the newspaper, having received the mistaken report that it was Albert that passed away, published the following obituary: "The 'merchant of death' is dead…Dr. Alfred Nobel, who became rich by finding ways to kill more people faster than ever before, died yesterday."

Realizing that this was not what he wanted to be remembered for, Nobel went on to invent a series of prizes for those who added something to benefit mankind in the areas of physics, chemistry, medicine, literature, and peace, leaving most of his assets to establish the five Nobel Prizes.

If we would write our own eulogy, what would it say? If we would write two eulogies—one, what people would say about us if we were to die today; and the other, the ideal eulogy about how we would like to be remembered—how would these two eulogies be different? And if we read our ideal eulogy every day, how would we be different?

Our Sages seemed to have thought about death a lot and encouraged us to do the same. In many places, the Sages advise one who needs motivation to hold back from unbecoming behavior to think about death. But rather than telling us to write our own eulogy, they encourage us to think about the afterlife.

This can be a very difficult task because we can't really envision what the afterlife will truly be like. Adding greater complication is that when we try to think about it, we find ourselves creating a Heavenly scene that is based on the various descriptions that we have heard that don't all quite line up—mixed together with images that are influenced by other religions, mixed together with some movie scenes—all leaving us utterly confused as to where we are all headed.

But that is not the idea. Our Sages are not telling us to try to entice ourselves by thinking about the pleasures of paradise or scare ourselves by imagining the fires of hell. They are teaching us that the key to living every moment fully is to envision that very moment that we move beyond the constraints of our corporeality and of this physical world and look at ourselves for what we truly are. No masks, no excuses, nothing to hide behind. No one left to impress or to prove anything to. When we exist in that reality of being in the presence of the Heavenly forum that will greet us in the Next World, in a state of absolute authenticity, how would we look at the life that we lived?

So, they encourage us, not to prepare our eulogy, but to prepare a short presentation of how we would describe the life we lived when we are in that all-knowing place. Now, they understood that you might need some additional instructions as to what you might be asked to speak about. So, they give us the following description of seven criteria that will be necessary for us to be deemed worthy in the Next World. As you read it, keep in mind that the purpose of the Rabbis' words is not to give you a play-by-play of the afterlife; it is to get you to think deeply about your life TODAY.

So, in order to really assure that we are mapping out a path to accomplish our mission in this world correctly, let's take a look at this piece from the Talmud together. It will give us a very specific picture of what we are supposed to be accomplishing in this world. As we explore the four elements, we will be referencing this piece together, unpacking each one in order to explore it in more detail, and showing how it relates to the lives of the Patriarchs and Matriarchs, and to each of the inner domains.

THE INTERVIEW

The Sages of the Talmud, commenting on the verse, "And the faith of your times shall be the strength of salvations, wisdom and knowledge, but fear of the Lord is his treasure,"[3] teach us the following:

> *After departing from this world, when a person is brought to judgment for the life he lived in this world, they say to him:*
>
> - *Did you conduct your business faithfully?*
> - *Did you designate times for Torah (i.e., did you designate time to work on your personal and spiritual growth)?*
> - *Did you engage in the commandment to be fruitful and multiply?*
> - *Did you hope for deliverance (from trouble)?*
> - *Did you engage in the discussions of wisdom?*
> - *Did you understand one matter from another (i.e., did you seek to fully explore the depth of the world's wisdom)?*
> - *And, beyond all these, if his treasure is his awe of God, yes (i.e., he is worthy), and if not, then he is not.*[4]

We will now go on a journey together and explore the path to empowerment. We will learn the various traits of greatness and how they relate to these seven criteria. We will see how they are embodied through

---

3   Isaiah 33:6.

4   Talmud, *Shabbos* 31a.

the various stories in the Book of Genesis, and we will learn how to be a human being who lives with the following:

- Boundless energy
- Selfless generosity
- Pleasure-filled, loving relationships
- Wellsprings of hope, no matter what challenges life brings
- Intellectual honesty
- Meaningful communication
- Humble, fearless leadership

summary

In this chapter, we discussed two critical components of the journey toward elevating the four elements and accomplishing our mission in this world:

1. The first is the attributes of our Patriarchs and Matriarchs. We will show how each generation excelled in specific areas that correspond to the four elements.
2. The second component is the seven achievements that we must account for in our Sages' version of the Heavenly interview in the afterlife. These, too, will connect back to the four elements, as we will see in the upcoming chapters.

7

EARTH (PART 1)— BOUNDLESS ENERGY

NEFESH LEVEL/ ELEMENT	OBSTACLES	HOW TO ELEVATE	PERSONIFIED BY
Body level/ Earth	Sluggishness Laziness Sadness Jealousy	Energy Joy Consistency of habit Abundance mindset	Abraham and Sarah (Rebecca)

And the angels run and return,
like the appearance of the sparks.

Ezekiel 1:14

IS YOUR BATTERY RUNNING LOW?

The most important icon on the screen of most electronic devices is the little battery icon that informs us how much power is left. So many of our emotions are linked to that icon, such as the anxiety it causes when it shows that our cell-phone battery is down to half-life but we still have several hours left before we will be able to charge up; or the victorious feeling when it is down to the last bar and we slide the charger into the socket just before it gets to the point of the device shutting down completely. We feel like a superhero rescuing a helpless victim only moments before it is too late.

One very clever advertisement for an energy dietary supplement featured a depiction of consumers before and after they used the product. Hovering right above the head of each consumer was an image that looked like the infamous battery icon. In the "before" frame, the icon is down to empty and the characters are looking tired, edgy, and disheveled. In the "after" frame, the characters have now become perky, relaxed, and put-together.

Imagine we all had such an icon hovering over our head. How many of us would say that our battery icon is typically showing full, and how many would say that we usually feel like we are running on empty? What about the people around us? Would you guess that their batteries are usually full?

Sometimes, we meet people who seem to be exploding with energy. They seem so full of life that the moment they walk into the room, the room seems to be electrified by their presence. They seem to be full of joy and a zest for life, a smile and a glow radiating from their faces that seems to overflow from their heart right into the hearts of whoever is around them. These are the people that everyone wants to be around. What is their secret?

In this chapter, we will speak about how to elevate the element of earth, which is connected to the physical body and is the root of sluggishness and sadness. Just like earth, which is stable and dense, the body/physical part of the *nefesh* is not naturally inclined toward action and spontaneity but rather toward making sure that there is stability and security in one's life. The negative outcome of this lack of enthusiasm is that it leads to laziness and lack of energy. But when used properly, it can also be a very powerful tool.

We quoted above the words of Rabbi Moshe Chaim Luzzatto, who said that the element of earth creates a downward pull and laziness. He gives us a remedy, though, how to overcome this:

> *Zeal can result from an inner passion, but it can also create one.*
> *That is, one who perceives a quickening of his outer movements*

*in the performance of a good deed conditions himself to expe-
rience a flaming inner movement through which longing and
desire will continually grow. If, however, he is sluggish in the
movement of his limbs, the movement of his spirit will die
down and be extinguished. Experience testifies to this.*[1]

Thus, we find that a person's earth element, i.e., their body, is not
only the problem, for it can provide the solution as well. When one uses
their outer movements in a way that displays life, joy, and excitement
to be alive, this creates "a flaming inner movement," feelings of energy,
vitality, and happiness.

ABRAHAM, SARAH, AND THE POWER OF MOVEMENT

The original patriarch and matriarch of the Jewish People are the
prototypes for such behavior.

Abraham and Sarah were prophets as well as dynamic teachers.
They are credited for their bravery to go out into a corrupted world
to preach and educate about monotheism and morality. Yet, we don't
hear too much detail in the Torah about their powerful seminars
and lectures that drew tens of thousands of dedicated followers (although we do know from Jewish tradition that this was indeed the
case).[2] There is some mention in passing about how when they set
out on their spiritual quest to the Land of Canaan, they did so with
an entourage of followers who had become like children to them.
But much of their success in the field of outreach is mentioned only
in passing.

However, when it comes to their enthusiasm and zest for life, the
Torah gives a very detailed and lengthy account. We can see these
traits shining through in the following Torah account that describes
the generosity of Abraham and Sarah, giving us very specific detail
about how they performed their hospitality:

---

1   *The Path of the Just*, chap. 7.
2   Maimonides, *Mishneh Torah*, Laws of Idolatry 1:3.

> *Looking up, he saw three men standing near him. As soon as he saw them, he **ran** from the entrance of the tent to greet them...Abraham **hastened** into the tent to Sarah and said, "**Quick**, take three seah of choice flour! Knead and make cakes!" Then Abraham **ran** to the herd, took a calf...and gave it to a servant who **hastened** to prepare it.[3]*

What we are witnessing here is nothing short of five-star service! Here, the spiritual giants of the generation are playing the role of maître d', chef, and waiter for their guests, and getting quite a workout in the process! The overall theme that we see in the story is the excitement and speed by which they serve, showing their true delight in having this opportunity to serve guests.

In Hebrew, the trait of enthusiasm is called *zerizus*. It is an essential trait for anyone in search of greatness. One thing that all high-performers have in common is the ability to move through their day with explosive energy, moving from task to task with precision and capitalizing on every moment. While most of society is sluggish and counting the minutes until they could have their next coffee break or check their social media, the Abrahams and Sarahs of the world have a bounce in their step from the moment that they wake up until the moment that they go to bed.

HABITS OF HIGHLY ENERGETIC PEOPLE

EXPRESS JOY

Because the earth element weighs us down, it can also cause us to feel sadness, sometimes without a real reason why. There is certainly no shortage of triggers in life that will bring us down, but very many times we are just feeling sad for no real reason. In order to validate why we are feeling this way, our mind will look for things in our life that are less than perfect and blame it on that, when in fact it is just the earth element at work.

---

3   Genesis 18:2–7.

Happiness and joy are crucial to self-mastery, to being the people we want to be, and to any sort of personal and spiritual growth. It affects almost everything else that will be discussed in this book, and depending on what is really causing the sadness, it will affect how we go about dealing with it. But there is at least one course of action that should be included in any plan to increase our happiness, and that is the external display of joy.

One who displays energetic outer movements will find that they feel more joy on the inside. This can include actual physical activity, like adjusting one's posture, increasing the pace that they are moving, doing exercise, singing and dancing, laughing, and even speaking about joyous subjects. Even if these actions are not coming naturally, pushing oneself to do these things will completely uplift a person's mood.

In fact, one of the most common pieces of advice given for anyone struggling with sadness or minor depression is to move their body and do outer movements that will ignite joy. As the saying goes, "Motion ignites emotion." When one smiles or laughs, feelings of inner joy are immediately ignited. There are even different therapies that exist where groups of people gather for the sole purpose of laughing together...about absolutely nothing!

The Hebrew word for face is "*panim*." The letters are actually the same as the word "*p'nim*," which means the inside, or essence, of something. We know that in the Hebrew language, when words are similar in their root, they must be similar in their essence. A person's face and the expression it displays is a window into what is going on inside that person. Feelings of pain, sadness, worry, or joy all display themselves through the various facial expressions. When a person smiles, their whole face expands, which means their inner world is expanding as well. When a person is upset, their face becomes constricted. Their lips lock, their eyes become smaller, and their whole face seems to tighten. This reflects the constriction that is happening inside of them.

WHEN A PERSON SMILES, THEIR WHOLE FACE EXPANDS, WHICH MEANS THEIR INNER WORLD IS EXPANDING AS WELL.

The Torah speaks about the importance of serving God with joy (Deuteronomy 28:47), and King David echoes this when he writes,

"Serve God with joy." Many great Jewish writers have written about joy, but perhaps no one is recognized as much for his teachings on the subject than the great Chassidic master, Rabbi Nachman of Breslov. In his writings, he emphasizes both the necessity of joy in all spiritual growth as well as the importance of external movements—such as singing, dancing, and clapping—to awaken joy within, especially when one is feeling down.

He writes that "It is a great mitzvah to always be happy." Addressing those who are struggling with sadness, he advises:

> *Strengthen yourself to push aside all depression and sadness. Everyone has lots of problems, and the nature of man is to be attracted to sadness. To escape these difficulties, constantly bring joy into your life—even if you have to resort to silliness.*[4]

The Talmud relates an episode about a great Sage who used to frequent the market where he would have mystical encounters with Elijah the Prophet. On one occasion, he asked Elijah to point out anyone in the market whose merit would guarantee them a place in the Next World. Elijah pointed out two individuals who, from their external appearance, did not necessarily look saintly at all. The Sage approached them and asked, "What is your occupation?"

They responded, "We are jesters. When we see sad people, we cheer them up, and when we see two people in an argument, we strive to make peace between them."[5]

We see from this story the incredible value of laughter and joy, and the tremendous merit in bringing joy to someone with laughter—defusing some of the stress in their life and helping them to see the world in a lighter way. Maybe this is why there is such an illustrious history of Jewish comedians!

And, perhaps, this is why the first people whom the Torah mentions as having laughed were Abraham and Sarah! Since Abraham and Sarah are the archetypes for uplifting the earth element using the power of

---

4   *Likutei Moharan* 2:24.
5   *Taanis* 22a.

movement, it is certainly appropriate that they, too, would be the ones to teach us the value of laughter.

One might wonder how it is possible for external motions to ignite joy if one is really sad on the inside. Isn't it just covering over the sadness that lies inside? Can external movements really make a sad person genuinely happy? The answer is that the potential for joy, just like sadness, exists inside everyone's heart, no matter what is happening in their life. The external circumstances that we face simply capture our attention and communicate to our inner world which emotion to unlock. Like the old Jewish saying goes: "Why do we have two pockets? One is filled with joy. The other is filled with sadness." If we do not actively direct our attention where to turn, we are allowing factors outside of ourselves to make that decision for us, and because of the earth element, it will gravitate toward what is sad. But through the external movements of joy, we are sending powerful messages to our inner world that it must unlock the wellsprings of joy that exist inside of us!

DAILY ROUTINES

Just like earth, which is stable and doesn't move, our inner earth element looks for stability and consistency in our life. Our emotions, thoughts, and motivations come and go, but the habit and routines that we institute in our life are perhaps the most dependable aspects in our life. In fact, modern research has shown that the most successful people on the planet—the high-level performers, the billionaires, the artists, the greatest athletes, and the high achievers—all share one thing in common: what has become referred to by popular lifestyle influencers as "success habits," the daily routines and rituals that they remain unwaveringly committed to.

Without routines and habits, we start feeling insecurity and anxiety, which leads to sadness and sluggishness. This is why people whose lives lack structure, either because of an unstructured job or lack of a job, are advised to institute set routines throughout their day to give them a sense of structure. When schools and businesses shut down in 2020 due to COVID-19 and the whole world felt disrupted and insecure, the most common piece of advice given was to create strong routines so as not to slide into a feeling of constant worry and fear.

Apparently, Abraham was a creature of habit as well. It is from him that our Sages learn the value of having a set place to pray, based on the verse, "And Abraham rose in the morning to the place where he had stood before God."[6] Not only do they emphasis having a set place where we carry out our spiritual tasks, but they also emphasized having set times for our prayer and for our Torah study.

One of the most important routines to develop revolves around the most crucial part of the day that will determine whether the day will be filled with energy or with sluggishness. And that is how we spend our mornings. The morning is a time when the element of earth is the strongest. This is why the slogan of many high performers is: "Conquer the morning. Conquer the day." The very opening words of the *Shulchan Aruch*, the Jewish code of law is: "One should strengthen himself like a lion to get up in the morning to serve his Creator so that it is he who awakens the dawn."

The Torah makes note that Abraham pushed himself to become a "morning person," mentioning on numerous occasions that "Abraham awoke early in the morning."[7] Our Sages echo this by telling us that Abraham established the morning as a time for prayer and instituted the morning prayer. Here, Abraham is teaching us that a person who awakens with enthusiasm and immediately infuses his day with spirituality is filling up their tank for the day and will draw from that energy as they move through the many draining tasks of that day.

STAY HEALTHY

Simple maintenance of our body is crucial in our state of joy and energy. Keeping our bodies healthy by eating properly, sleeping enough, and exercising frequently can make a huge difference in our overall performance. The Torah states: "Take utmost care and watch yourselves

---

6   Genesis 19:27.

7   Ibid. 19:27, 22:3.

scrupulously," which the commentaries explain as referring to one's physical health.[8]

The great Sage Maimonides, who was also a doctor, writes: "Bodily health and well-being are part of the path to God, for it is impossible to understand or have any knowledge of the Creator when one is sick. Therefore, one must avoid anything that may harm the body, and one must cultivate healthful habits."[9]

This idea is echoed by Rabbi Moshe Chaim Luzzatto in his book *Derech Hashem*:

> *One of the commandments requires that we keep our bodies fit so that we can serve God, and that we derive our needs from the environment to achieve this goal. In this manner, we elevate ourselves even through such activities. The world itself is also elevated, since it is then also helping man to serve God.[10]*

The Torah does not tell us about Abraham and Sarah's approach to health. But what is fascinating to note is that it is specifically Abraham who is recognized for spiritually elevating every aspect of his earthly body. Our Sages, in their deeper analysis of the Torah, use a tool called *gematria*, numerology. Using this tool, they understand the deeper significance of an event based on the numerical value of the letters in a word or phrase.

Throughout their writing, when our Sages speak about the number of limbs in the human body, they consistently refer to them as the 248 limbs of the body.[11] Fascinatingly enough, the Hebrew letters of the name Abraham equal 248 (A-V-R-H-M = 1+2+200+5+40). It is as if his very name shows that he was the master over all of his physical

---

8   *Brachos* 32b. See also *Path of the Just* 10:5.

9   Maimonides, *Mishneh Torah*, Laws of Attributes 4:1.

10   *The Way of God* 1:4:7.

11   The Mishnah (*Ohalos* 1:8) lists the 248 limbs (bones) in a person: 30 in the foot (six in each toe), 10 in the ankle, 2 in the shin, 5 in the knee, 1 in the thigh, 3 in the pelvis, 11 ribs, 30 in the hand (6 in each finger), 2 in the forearm, 2 in the elbow, 1 in the upper arm, and 4 in the shoulder. (This makes 101 on one side and 101 on the other.) 18 vertebrae in the spine, 9 in the head, 8 in the neck, 6 in the "opening to the heart," and 5 in the orifices.

body, implying self-mastery over his earth element.[12] Perhaps it is the mastery of the earth element that is being hinted to in the fact that Abraham is the Torah personality who refers to himself using the term "I am but earth and ashes."[13]

summary

We have seen how our external movements are the key to self-mastery over the earth element and the negative traits of sluggishness and sadness. Included in this is

- a quickening of one's movement, including the pace that we walk and the posture that we hold;
- joyous external movements, including smiling, laughing, singing, dancing, and even humor;
- set routines and habits, especially a set morning routine;
- keeping the body healthy through eating and exercising.

---

12   See *Rashi* on Genesis 17:1.

13   Genesis 18:27.

8

EARTH (PART 2)— THE ABUNDANCE MINDSET

NEFESH LEVEL/ ELEMENT	OBSTACLES	HOW TO ELEVATE	PERSONIFIED BY
Body level/ Earth	Sluggishness Laziness Sadness Jealousy	Energy Joy Consistency of habit Abundance mindset	Abraham and Sarah (Rebecca)

Think good and it will be good.

The Lubavitcher Rebbe

THE EXPANDING SELF

In the previous chapter, we explored how the earth element inside of us is the root of sluggishness and sadness. We now turn our attention to the other struggle that is rooted in the element of earth: jealousy, as we saw in the story of Cain killing Abel. This is because jealousy is a direct result of a feeling of lowliness and lack of self-esteem. When we feel insecure about ourselves, we create a narrative in our mind that everyone else's success is coming at our expense. Since the earth element is primarily about survival and security, when we feel threatened by other people, it arouses all sorts of negative emotions against them.

In contrast to the story of Cain and Abel, Abraham and Sarah are famous for their generosity and giving. In that sense, they rectified the flaw of jealousy. Rather than viewing other people as a threat to themselves, they viewed others as an extension of themselves. And because of that, the very same earth element that is connected to survival and security caused them to be concerned about the sustenance of everyone else, whom they viewed as a part of themselves. This is why they opened up inns where they would feed people and offer them lodging.[1]

It is for this reason that Abraham and Sarah were the first ones to be driven to proactively go out and teach monotheism to the world, even though they were certainly not the first people to believe in one God. Abraham and Sarah understood a secret about God that none of the other prophets that came before them knew. They realized that belief in God was not complete until one sees the spark of Godliness that is all around them, especially in the hearts of the people around them. It is only then that they can fully embrace their life and rejoice in it and share that with the people around them.

They discovered that every single person, no matter how far they drifted, still has a glowing ember inside that just needed to be stoked with warmth and kindness. Their kindness was not simply because they were nice people who enjoyed hosting guests but because they were able to see that God doesn't only exist in Heaven. He exists on Earth in the heart of every human being. Abraham and Sarah discovered God in a place that was truly unknown to those who preceded them.

---

1   Genesis 21:33.

We must ask, then, how can one take the earth element that naturally creates a feeling of jealousy and turn it into a source of generosity and feeling of responsibility for others?

HABITS OF EXPANSIVE PEOPLE

THE OUTER MOVEMENTS OF GENEROSITY

We mentioned above that proper usage of the earth element, like energetic outer movements, smiling, and exercise, can ignite joy and energy inside of us. This same concept is true about generosity as well. Just as joy is ignited with outer movements, so too are feelings of generosity and love. When a person is in a state of joy, the natural response is to want to bring joy to others. Therefore we can observe a chain reaction of enthusiasm leading to joy, which then brings to love, which, in turn, translates into generosity. This is why the Torah specifically chooses to teach us about the trait of enthusiasm in the context of Abraham and Sarah's hospitality.

In the story of Cain, the worker of the earth, his face fell, his frown triggered a thickening of his earth element. When the earth element is used to weigh a person down, they experience sadness and jealousy. But when the earth element is turned upward, it awakens energy and enthusiasm and becomes a vessel for feelings of love and connection.

This is not the only time that the Torah connects enthusiasm with hospitality. When we first meet the daughter-in-law of Abraham and Sarah, the matriarch Rebecca, she is drawing water from a well when she is approached by Abraham's servant who had just been traveling in the hot desert. In that episode we see an echoing of the hospitality of Abraham and Sarah:

> She **quickly** lowered her jug upon her hand and let him drink.
> When she had let him drink his fill, she said, "I will also draw
> for your camels, until they finish drinking." **Quickly** emptying
> her jug into the trough, she **ran** back to the well to draw, and
> she drew for all his camels.[2]

---

2   Ibid. 24:18–20.

This account of Rebecca's generosity, which sounds almost identical to the style of Abraham and Sarah, emphasizes this point: that feelings of generosity go hand-in-hand with the outer gestures of enthusiasm and energy.[3] In fact, Jewish tradition teaches that a big act of kindness done with lack of energy and a sour attitude toward the recipient is not as great as a smaller act of kindness that is done with warmth and love.

THE SCARCITY MINDSET VS. ABUNDANCE MINDSET

Many studies have shown how the mind shapes reality, and what we believe to be true will manifest itself in our life. In modern popular psychology, they call it the law of attraction or universal magnetism. Judaism calls it *emunah*. Emunah is very often translated as "faith," but this translation doesn't do it justice. Faith sounds like something purely passive and theoretical belief in something that one can't really fully know. *Emunah*, on the other hand, is a mindset that actively shapes reality. The power of the mind believing that something will happen is so strong that it becomes a channel for Divine potential to manifest into actuality.

THE POWER OF THE MIND BELIEVING THAT SOMETHING WILL HAPPEN IS SO STRONG THAT IT BECOMES A CHANNEL FOR POTENTIAL TO MANIFEST INTO ACTUALITY.

The actual root of the word *emunah* is *omein*, a craft, something that is brought into reality through the hands of a craftsman. It shares a root with the Hebrew word *ima*, mother, who brings life from potential into actuality. This all points to the fact that there is a tremendous power in positive thinking, because our beliefs have the power to tap into what exists only in potential and "birth it" into reality.

Therefore, part of the mindset that we are supposed to develop in this lifetime is that there is an abundance in the world that is available to us. The Almighty has all of the resources necessary to provide for the entire world. The success of others does

---

3   We must point out as well that the Hebrew letters that make up the name *Rivkah* (Rebecca) are *reish, beis, kuf, hei*, which are the same letters that make up the word *ha'boker*, the morning. We showed in the last chapter that waking up early in the morning was a habit that was also related to Abraham.

not in any way minimize the potential for one to be successful. On the contrary, when we see someone else's success, it should open our eyes to the great abundance that God has and is ready to give, of which we too can be the recipients.

If our mindset is focused on scarcity, then it is scarcity that we will manifest. If we are always worried and anxious because we believe that there is a shortage of resources, money, and success to go around, then that is what we will experience. However, if we internalize and live with the belief that there is an abundance that is available to us, then we are attracting that abundance and blessing toward us.

Our trust that God wants the best for us and is ready to rain down blessing upon us shapes our reality. This is what is meant in Psalms when it says, "God is your shadow."[4] There is an abundance of blessing that is set aside for each of us in our "Heavenly bank accounts." It is more than what we need to live the life of abundance and to enable us to accomplish our mission. All of the effort that we are putting in to make a livelihood is just for the sake of unlocking what is already prepared for us. When we go about our business dealings with serenity and a positive attitude, we are unlocking that abundance. When we have a constricted attitude, we are also constricting the pipelines through which the Divine blessing will flow.

The Torah says specifically by Abraham that he merited tremendous blessing "[because] he put his *emunah* in God, so [God] considered it to his merit."[5] When we live with the *emunah*/abundance mindset, we behave in a different way. We are more generous with our loved ones, with our charity, and with people who serve us. We eliminate from our life a lot of the worry, tension, and anxiety that revolves around money, and our success is reflected in that. Our resources become like an electric current in that the more we let the current flow, the more that it will perpetuate, but the more that we constrict it, the less power it has. Our relationship toward money will determine the role that money will play in our life.

---

4   Psalms 21:5.

5   Genesis 15:6.

GET PAID TO GIVE, NOT TO TAKE

We mentioned above that Cain was "a worker of the earth." While this can simply mean that the earth was what he was working on, we can also homiletically interpret it that he was a worker with an "earth mentality," meaning a constricted mentality. Because of that, the focus of his work was for him to take whatever he could. The name Cain shares a root with the Hebrew word *kinyan*, an acquisition. That was the entire focus of his work—to see how much materialism he could acquire.

Though part of being human is working in order to sustain ourselves, the focus of our work is still supposed to be about becoming a giver and not a taker. This means that we see ourselves in a giving role in that we are helping the people whom we serve and making the world a better place with our service. Yes, we need to be compensated so that we can afford to properly serve, but that does not change the fact that the overall motivation behind our work should be that we are trying to assist others and create a better world. If we are being paid for our services, that means that we are serving a need, which means that we will have many opportunities to make a difference in people's lives—in a direct or indirect way.

When we view ourselves in a giving role, everything about our day is infused with more energy and blessing. We become more productive with our time and are more motivated to go beyond the call of duty. The way we treat people we work with improves, and we are better equipped to handle frustration and failure. We become more fearless in how we approach potential customers or clients, and we don't take rejection as personally because we genuinely believe that we are serving the client and helping them improve their lives. We also find that we begin to care more about the person we are doing business with. To quote Winston Churchill: "We make a living by what we get. We make a life by what we give."

Our Sages say that the greatest attribute is having a good reputation.[6] In business, this means becoming a deeply trustworthy person who

---

6   *Ethics of Our Fathers* 4:12.

cares not only about one's self, but also about the people that he is doing business with.

The great investor and philanthropist Warren Buffett is famous for cutting major deals with just a handshake. In a world where every deal needs to be handled by several lawyers with pages and pages of contracts, Buffett's good name is so powerful that a mere handshake is enough to let the other know that he will come through.

In contrast to the attitude of Cain, Abraham believed that his role was to be a giver and to minimize what he took from others as much as possible. Even when offered a reward for his services, Abraham swore that he would not accept "even a thread to a shoe strap."[7]

Abraham is also the only Biblical personality of whom the Torah gives a glimpse of his actual business dealings. After twelve chapters in the Torah discussing the many adventures of Abraham and Sarah, the final tale of Abraham is his purchase of the Cave of Machpelah in Hebron for the burial of his deceased wife, Sarah. Once again, we see Abraham refusing to be in the role of a taker. When offered the chance to name his price, Abraham responds, "Let him give it to me for full price," showing that he is definitely *not* the person that you would take along to back you up in your real estate negotiations.

This final peek into the life of Abraham is amazing for another reason. Take note of the specific nature of this business deal. It was over a *piece of land* that would be used as a burial place; meaning, it was a business deal revolving around the element of earth!

But there is more. In this final story of Abraham, we are literally seeing a complete reversal of the story of Cain killing Abel. That story also involved a burial. But there it was the burial of Abel, when the ground "swallowed up" Abel's blood, covering up the sin of Cain, for which it was cursed (symbolizing the struggle of the earth element). Now, in the final story of Abraham, he is purchasing a plot of land to bury his wife in his signature style of generosity

---

7   Genesis 14:23.

and abundance. The Torah is showing that the element of earth has now been elevated and redeemed.

The verse confirms this by using a peculiar language when describing the status of the field after it was purchased by Abraham, stating that it "rose to Abraham as his possession."[8] Our Sages comment: "It received a rise in importance because it passed from the possession of a commoner into the possession of a king."[9] We know that this plot of land, the cave of Machpeila in the city of Hebron, is now considered one of the holiest sites in all of Israel.

The symbolism in these words is that just like this plot of earth became elevated by entering into Abraham's possession, the same holds true for our element of earth. When we embody the traits of Abraham, we take hold of the element of earth and transform our laziness, sadness, and jealousy into energy, joy, and loving-kindness!

THE OPENING QUESTIONS IN THE WORLD TO COME

Before we complete our discussion about the earth element, let's take a look at the second component of the road to greatness that we spoke about above—the "Post-Game Interview," the criteria for which we will have to show as our souls stand at the gates of Heaven in the afterlife. Let's examine the first two questions that are asked of us and see how we are doing.

QUESTION #1: DID YOU CONDUCT YOUR WORK WITH EMUNAH?

There are two common ways to understand the term "with *emunah*." The first is "faithful to the people that you are doing business with." The second is "faithful to God."

Though these are two different interpretations, we see how they go hand-in-hand. We described in this chapter how when a person has faith in God, they live with an abundance mindset which completely

---

8   Ibid. 23:17.
9   *Bereishis Rabbah* 58:8 (quoted in *Rashi*, Genesis 23:17).

changes their relationship toward money and business. With an abundance mindset, we will naturally earn the faith of the people we engage with in business, because they know that they will be taken care of and can expect quality and honesty.

We all intuitively know whether the person that we are dealing with is just looking to make a sale or whether they really have our best interest in mind. I remember attending the funeral of one of the great philanthropists in the Washington, DC, area. One of the sons, who had taken over the family business, spoke about how when he took over the business, he asked his father for the best piece of advice he had for him. His response was, "Whenever you are doing a deal, you need to make sure of two things: that you are getting a good deal, and that the other guy is getting a good deal too." That is truly an expression of doing our business faithfully.

QUESTION #2: DID YOU DESIGNATE TIMES FOR TORAH?

This question focuses on whether we established habits that would help us grow spiritually. In chapter 12, we will discuss the specific merits of Torah study, which will also be the subject of more of the questions in the "interview," but at this point the question is specifically focusing on the habits, the "designated times" that we created.

As we said above, the earth element inside us looks for stability and routine. If it isn't part of a routine or habit, the earth element will push back with resistance in the form of laziness and sluggishness. Therefore, any area of personal or spiritual growth will require strong habits that are deeply embedded into our inner wiring. In this way, we are using the earth element to our favor, rather than trying to overcome it.

We spoke about the tendency for those who have achieved mastery in the struggles within the earth element to wake up early and use their mornings when they are fresh to accomplish those areas of personal/spiritual growth that would otherwise be neglected. It is not uncommon to find the most growth-oriented people in the early hours of the morning at the gym, in the synagogue, or engaged in early-morning reading, writing, reflecting, and studying. They know that if you conquer the morning, you will conquer the day and the element of earth.

summary

We have seen how generosity and expanding oneself to include others are keys to self-mastery over the earth element and the negative traits of jealousy. Included in this is

- performing acts of kindness with quickness and with joy;
- developing an abundance mindset, which will manifest itself in reality;
- viewing your job as an opportunity for you to become a giver rather than a taker.

9

WATER (PART 1)— LOVE VS. LUST

NEFESH LEVEL/ ELEMENT	OBSTACLES	HOW TO ELEVATE	PERSONIFIED BY
Feeling level/ Water	Lust	Channeled pleasure Deep love Hope	Isaac and Rebecca

Vast floods cannot quench the love,
nor can rivers drown it.

Song of Songs 8:7

IMAGINE THE FOLLOWING SCENARIO: A table is set in an empty room with two chairs on each side of the table. On the table, there is a lavish smorgasbord of delicacies, set on the finest dishes. The door opens and in walk two holy men, spiritual masters of their respective religions and practices. You are the server.

Each holy man sits down in one of the chairs. You approach Holy Man #1, who smiles at you with a face that is full of warmth and a glowing countenance, and you stack his plate high with layers of delicious food. He nods at you and thanks you for your service. He then closes his eyes and seems to go into some sort of trance. His lips are moving, and he seems to be mumbling some sort of mantra, blessing or words of grace.

You then begin to serve Holy Man #2, who looks at you with his sharp eyes and an I-mean-business look on his face, and raises his hand as if to tell you to stop. He then asks you to only put a spoonful of rice and two peas on his plate. He then goes on to explain to you that his diet only allows for the most minimal pleasure from this material world.

As this is going on, you turn back to Holy Man #1, who has now began enjoying a juicy piece of steak. His eyes are still closed. He is concentrating on every bite, a huge smile plastered across his face. He seems to be glowing with appreciation for each bite and at random intervals will blurt out some sort of affirmation that seems to be an expression of gratitude. All this, while Holy Man #2 is taking small bites of his rice, showing no signs of any enjoyment.

The two finish their food, and you clear their plates, utterly amazed at how two different spiritual paths can have such diametrically opposed attitudes toward physical pleasure.

Indeed, physical pleasure, the human attribute that is most connected with the inner element of water, and religion seem to have a love/hate relationship. We are aware that holy men in many religions abstain from many physical pleasures. They minimize their food intake to the very basics and keep sexual activity to a minimum, if not withdrawing completely. Some religious practitioners even sleep on hard mattresses to minimize their comfort in the world. Their belief is that the more one removes themselves from worldly pleasures, the more one will be able to activate the more subtle inner experiences and awaken their spiritual nature.

What is Judaism's view of pleasure?

If we look in traditional Jewish texts, we see hints toward both pathways. We find many statements from our Sages referring to a life of separation and abstinence. The most significant of them is:

> *Such is the way [of a life] of Torah: you shall eat bread with*
> *salt, and rationed water shall you drink; you shall sleep on the*

ground, your life will be one of privation, and in Torah shall you labor.[1]

On the other hand, we are well-aware that Jewish celebrations, especially Shabbat and the holidays, are filled with delicacies, wine, and fine garments. Consider this quote from one of the Shabbat songs:

Eat delicacies, drink sweet drinks, for God provides for all who show devotion,

Clothes to wear, plentiful bread, meat, fish, and all sorts of delicious foods.[2]

So how does one reconcile these two paths? How can we live both a life of abstinence but also a life of pleasure? How can we live on both bread and salt and also enjoy our delicacies?

To answer this question, we turn to the next section of the book of Genesis and meet the second Patriarch and Matriarch—Isaac and Rebecca.

ISAAC: CONQUEROR OR CONNOISSEUR?

Let us first look at the trait of Isaac. Our Sages teach us that the trait of Isaac is a trait called *gevurah*, translated as inner strength or discipline. To understand this trait, we turn back to our Sages in *Ethics of Our Fathers*, who teach us: "Who is considered a person of strength? One who has learned to conquer their desires."[3]

To conquer one's desires does not mean making them go away. It means having them under your control to use them however you would like. When an army conquers a city, the greatest expression of strength is not to destroy the enemy. It is to take them under their control. That is true *gevurah*.[4]

TO CONQUER ONE'S DESIRES DOES NOT MEAN MAKING THEM GO AWAY. IT MEANS HAVING THEM UNDER YOUR CONTROL TO USE THEM HOWEVER YOU WOULD LIKE.

---

1   *Ethics of Our Fathers* 6:4.
2   *Yom Zeh Mechubad.*
3   Ibid. 4:1.
4   The generation that corrupted the element of pleasure was the generation of the flood. Their

The two polarities that we mentioned before—abstinence and pleasure—can be observed in the life of Isaac.

> Isaac is identified by a seminal moment in his life when, at the age of thirty-seven, he was ready and willing to be brought as an offering to God. The Sages expound on his readiness to give himself up completely for God by adding that he encouraged his father by saying, "Bind me tighter." The image of him being bound and ready to sacrifice everything is a symbol of complete nullification of the self.
>
> Amazingly enough, the Torah also makes frequent mention of Isaac's affinity for physical pleasure. We are told that Isaac loved Esau more because "he put hunted food in his mouth."[5] Then, at the end of his life, Isaac once again calls upon Esau to "prepare a dish for me such as I like, and bring it to me to eat so that I may give you my innermost blessing before I die." It would seem that even Isaac enjoyed a tasty and succulent meal, as Rebecca tells Jacob a few verses later: "Go to the flock and fetch me two choice goats, and I will make of them a dish for your father, such as he likes."

It is neither contradiction nor coincidence that the Torah paints a picture of Isaac as one who is self-negating but also one who appreciates the finer things, just as it is no contradiction to follow both of the paths that we mentioned previously.

The Jewish path is one that encourages a life full of happiness and pleasure. It is a great misconception of many who believe that the Torah is full of rules and regulations that are somehow supposed to limit the pleasure that we are supposed to have in this life. But Judaism does teach that in order to maximize our pleasure in this world, we need to develop the ability to be in control of our desires and not that our

---

punishment was complete destruction. The name Isaac, which in Hebrew is pronounced Yitzchak, has the Hebrew letters *yud, tzaddi, ches,* and *kuf,* the very same letters that make up the Hebrew words *keitz chai*—the end of life.

5   Genesis 25:28. While the Sages interpret this homiletically to mean that he trapped him with deceptive questions, one still has to ask what the Torah is hinting to in its simple reading. See *Shabbos* 63a—"Ein mikra yotzei mi'dei peshuto."

desires are in control of us. When we become the conqueror of our desires, we are now able to channel those pleasures so that it can work for us in the best possible way.

It is true that this goal of elevating our physical pleasures will require us, from time to time, to say no to certain activities that seem enticing for the moment. But so does a healthy diet. And, if you are a parent, I hope that you also tell your kids "no" quite often, even though they really, really want to stay up late and play video games, with a Slurpee and gummy bears, on a school night.

IN ORDER TO MAXIMIZE OUR PLEASURE IN THIS WORLD, WE NEED TO DEVELOP THE ABILITY TO BE IN CONTROL OF OUR DESIRES AND NOT THAT OUR DESIRES ARE IN CONTROL OF US.

The path of elevation encourages us to reframe how we look at pleasure and try to turn it into a growth experience. So, instead of engaging in a physically pleasurable activity just for the sake of the pleasure that we get from it, we try to develop a mindset as to what we are really achieving through that activity. Some of the ways we can be more mindful is to focus on the following:

- How this pleasure will give us good health or energy
- How it might strengthen us physically, emotionally, or mentally
- How it will give us the ability to appreciate the Almighty for the gift of pleasure
- How we are utilizing and transforming the raw materials of creation into sources of strength so that we can become the best version of us and serve God better

LOVE IS LIKE WATER

We mentioned previously that physical pleasure is represented by water, but water is also a symbol for authentic emotional connection. We showed how the generation of the flood made no boundaries whatsoever for their lust and became addicted to pursuing their physical desires. They were therefore destroyed by water. Lust, like water, destroys when it has no boundaries, but water channeled and directed properly is the source of all blessings. This is when we channel our desires and invest them into a deep, loving, and lasting relationship.

It is certainly befitting, then, that Isaac marries Rebecca, a woman who personifies, perhaps more than anyone else in the Torah, a deeply sensitive, caring, and loving individual.

> This is evident in our initial introduction to Rebecca, chosen as a wife for Isaac because of her kindness and care to all creatures. Perhaps we can make the case that it is no coincidence that when we first meet Rebecca in the Torah, she is performing her kindness at, you guessed it, a well of water.
>
> And it is certainly appropriate that when Isaac marries Rebecca, the description of his feelings toward her are from the most warm and intimate that we find in all of Torah. Of all the characters in the Torah, one might not expect that Isaac would be the one you would write a love story about. Yet, after meeting his wife Rebecca, the Torah describes a very deep love that Isaac has for her.
>
>> *Isaac then brought her into the tent of his mother Sarah, and he took Rebecca as his wife. Isaac loved her, and thus found comfort after his mother's death.*[6]
>
> It is also noteworthy that we don't hear very many incidents about Isaac and Rebecca's life, but the Torah goes into great detail to describe the issues Isaac had with the Philistines over digging wells and finding water. The Torah is emphasizing this point—that one who learns the art of inner discipline and restraint will be the one who will experience the deepest love and sensuality.

The symbolism of water representing deep, loving relationships teaches us many lessons. Water has just two elements: oxygen and hydrogen. When they come together, they create something new: water, the foundation of life. But the only reason that those elements combine is because of their polarity. The beauty of love is when two individuals come together—not for selfish reasons or to indulge in their own

---

6   Genesis 24:67.

benefits but for the specific desire of completing the other. It is also the movement and flexibility of water that symbolizes the flexibility of both parties that allows them to grow together. Water easily mixes and seamlessly becomes one unit. It is the water part of us that allows us to become one with another.

HABITS OF A TRUE LOVER

SEEING THE OTHER AS AN EXTENSION OF YOU

This is a proverb that further draws a parallel between love and water: "As face reflects the face in water, so does one's heart to another."[7] When we see our reflection in water, we realize that we are looking at ourselves. Successful relationships happen as we begin to see the other as a part of us. On a body level, we might be two separate people, but on a soul level, we are connected. The other's growth is my growth, his or her pain is my pain, etc. The transformation of lust to love happens when we no longer see ourselves as separate entities but as one and the same. Until then, one will still prioritize their own self-interests. A relationship that is centered on what each partner benefits is a relationship that can be easily uprooted when an outside object of lust presents itself.

THE BEAUTY OF LOVE IS WHEN TWO INDIVIDUALS COME TOGETHER—NOT FOR SELFISH REASONS OR TO INDULGE IN THEIR OWN BENEFITS BUT FOR THE SPECIFIC DESIRE OF COMPLETING THE OTHER.

If you have ever taken a tour of the major tourists sites in Israel, you might have heard your tour guide point out that the difference between the Sea of Galilee (which is full with living organisms) and the Dead Sea (which kills anything that tries to live in it) is that the Sea of Galilee overflows its waters into the Jordan, which goes on to water much of Israel. The Dead Sea, on the other hand, only receives incoming waters but does not feed its water out to any other source.

---

7   Proverbs 27:19.

The waters of love, too, only thrive when they overflow outward in a giving motion. When they are only flowing in, they are waters of lust, which inevitably die.

EMOTIONAL MIRRORING

The true lover understands yet another secret based on the reflecting power of water and of the heart, and that is the power of emotional mirroring. This means that we all have the ability to change the trajectory of a relationship purely by changing what is in our hearts. The relationship thrives when any one of the two partners decides in their heart to become more committed, more devoted, and more invested—even if it begins as a unilateral commitment. It isn't long before those feelings are reflected in the heart of the other. The relationship can also be sabotaged when one of the parties decides that they want to control, criticize, and change the other.

> WE ALL HAVE THE ABILITY TO CHANGE THE TRAJECTORY OF A RELATIONSHIP PURELY BY CHANGING WHAT IS IN OUR HEARTS.

If in my heart I haven't chosen to love and appreciate my spouse for who they are, or if I am just trying to change my spouse, even if I am saying all the right things and going through all the right motions, my heart is not sending the same message as my words and actions; this, too, will be felt in the relationship. Most relationships that are stuck boil down to the fact that each party is only willing to invest if they see reciprocation from the other, which can often leave the relationship at an emotional stalemate.

When one spouse chooses to love more, those feelings will eventually be aroused in the other spouse. When one spouse chooses to believe in the other more, the other spouse will eventually earn that belief. When one spouse chooses to respect the other more, even if they don't deserve it, that respect will eventually be earned.

PLEASURE CHANNELED PROPERLY

When the waters of love are flowing, then the waters of physical pleasure, romance, and intimacy also become waters of blessing. It is the fulfillment of the Torah's instruction to "cleave to her; become one flesh." The Divine Presence resides among a couple who are connecting simultaneously on a physical, emotional, and inevitably spiritual level. No wonder the Holy of Holies in the Temple was called "the chamber of beds," and the image of the male and female cherubs that resided there could be found in an embrace!

But the waters of blessings can only flow when the waters of lust have been properly channeled. Many relationships have been lost because the stolen waters of lust that seeped in from outside overtook the relationship's sweet waters of the love. The key is to look deeply into one's heart and realize that although the object of one's lust might seem beyond tempting at the moment, it is really love and connection that we so crave. We can dig deep into our emotions and draw from the endless wellspring of love that flows inside of us.

THE CONSTANT STRUGGLES OF THE EARTH AND WATER ELEMENTS

The struggles of sadness that relate to the element of earth and the struggles of temptation that relate to the element of water affect the lives of so many. We have suggested some approaches to achieve self-mastery in these areas. We have suggested that in order to overcome sadness, one should make it a habit to use one's body in a joyful and healthy way, as well as to establish empowering daily habits. We have shown that all lust is rooted in the desire for love, and that one should try to elevate their temptations by being mindful of why we are engaging in this pleasure, as well as trying to fill the natural need with deep, loving relationships.

It is important to emphasize that so much of our life's mission revolves around surmounting the struggles that are connected to these two obstacles. When we speak of mastery, it is important to remember that mastery looks different for different people. Few can say that they have mastered these struggles to the point that they no longer exist. Everybody struggles, and everybody falls sometimes. For most of us, mastery means that we are committed to the struggle and that we are constantly working to develop mechanisms to navigate through the lows and bounce back.

We must also remember that one who is struggling in any of these areas should never view themselves as inferior to other people. On the contrary, if this is where you struggle, then this is the mission that you have been chosen for, and you should consider it a symbol of greatness. As the great Chassidic master Rav Tzadok said, as we mentioned previously: "In the areas that a person struggles and repeatedly falls, it is in those areas that he is destined for greatness."[8]

As a rabbi, I so often encounter some of the most sincere and wonderful individuals who are struggling with some of the darkest and demoralizing habits and addictions. I have spoken to individuals who so badly want to do what's right and who yearn so strongly for spirituality yet are caught in a web of destructive behavior that seems to contradict their true desire. Rather than seeing it as a contradiction, though, we must realize that sometimes it is specifically the most sensitive souls that are vulnerable to these habits because of how intensely they experience their feelings and their emotions.

SOMETIMES IT IS SPECIFICALLY THE MOST SENSITIVE SOULS THAT ARE VULNERABLE TO THESE HABITS BECAUSE OF HOW INTENSELY THEY EXPERIENCE THEIR FEELINGS AND THEIR EMOTIONS.

Great people who care deeply about the world, who naturally feel love for the people that they encounter, who search for spirituality, who think and express themselves differently and creatively, often possess a much more profound awareness of the world and the people around them. The intensity of that awareness takes a toll on their emotions, and very often by default their emotional fatigue can push them toward intense sadness or to whatever coping mechanism they can easily access.

One who struggles with sadness or temptation should be aware that the struggle might be an indication as to the true depth of the person's soul. As one learns to properly channel these aspects of the inner world properly, one will find that their greatness will shine through beyond limits.

---

8   *Tzidkas Hatzaddik* §49.

summary

We have seen how channeling our pleasure is key to self-mastery over the water element and the negative traits of indulgence in temptation and lust. Included in this is

- minimizing pleasure for pleasure's sake alone and becoming mindful of why we are engaging in that pleasure;
- developing very deep and loving relationships that are built on growth, flexibility, and becoming one;
- gaining awareness and utilizing the power of emotional mirroring so that the inner state of your loved ones reflects your inner state for the positive and for the negative;
- staying positive no matter how deep you fall in any of the struggles of the earth and water elements.

10

WATER (PART 2)— PLANTING THE SEEDS OF YOUR LEGACY

NEFESH LEVEL/ ELEMENT	OBSTACLES	HOW TO ELEVATE	PERSONIFIED BY
Feeling level/ Water	Lust	Channeled pleasure Deep love Hope	Isaac and Rebecca

The offspring of the righteous
are their good deeds.

Rashi, Genesis 6:9

THE LIFE-GIVING POWER OF WATER

Deep, loving relationships are the true desire of the inner element of water and the corresponding emotional level of the *nefesh*. It is the greatest form of pleasure possible. The loving relationship that is formed in the context of a marriage can become the greatest experience of that pleasure. In order to continue growing that love and growing our capacity to love, we move to the next aspect of our mission in this world, which is still within the element of water, and that is to bring children into the world and to raise them with love and affection.

The natural outgrowth of sharing a deep love with one's spouse is to want to grow that love by uniting as one to bring another human being into the world and start a family. The act of procreation solidifies our oneness and creates an eternal bond. It is important to mention right off the bat that because having actual biological children is not a possibility for everyone, the themes discussed in this chapter are not limited to biological children, as we will see shortly.

The life-giving power of water represents our ability to bring life into the world.[1] It is truly wonderful, then, when we reflect upon the brilliance of God's creation—that the very same act of intimacy that can either be either denigrated to an act of lust or elevated as an expression of love, is the very same act that will bring a new life into the world. It is as if the Almighty is conveying to us that the process of elevating our inner element of water by turning lust into love is taken to even greater heights when that love turns into a source for new life.

We mentioned above that the first time that the Torah discusses the deep love that exists between husband and wife is in the context of Isaac and Rebecca. The very next time the Torah discusses Isaac and Rebecca, we find them praying together and yearning for a child. Rebecca was not the first woman in the Torah with fertility struggles; it took Sarah many years until she had Isaac. But the emphasis on the deep yearning to have children is found first in this instance.[2]

---

1 The Talmud (*Taanis* 2a) relates that "three keys God retained in His own hands and did not entrust them to the hand of any messenger, namely, the key of rain (water), the key of childbirth, and the key of the revival of the dead." The connection between rain and the lifegiving force of childbirth is also emphasized in the second blessing of the daily *Amidah* prayer. The main theme of the blessings is God's ability to give life and to restore life, yet inserted into that prayer is a line of gratitude for rain.

2 Not surprising then, that the blessing discussed in the previous footnote that discusses water and childbirth begins with the words, "*Atah Gibor*," You are mighty, which is symbolic of the trait of Isaac. Furthermore, the very words "*mechalkel chayim*," You sustain all life, has the numerical value of the Hebrew word Yitzchak (Isaac), both equaling 208.

The important role that having children plays in accomplishing one's life mission is evident in that it is the first mitzvah given in the Torah, i.e., to "be fruitful and multiply." The Torah is putting upon us not only the responsibility to populate the world, but to build a legacy for ourselves by raising children who will carry on the values that we pass on to them through our teaching and role modeling.[3]

It is important to note that one does not fulfill their mission by simply adding numbers to the human population, but rather by taking an active role in building the next generation of human beings who will continue to repair the world and add to it with their own individual expression so that they can continue the chain. The responsibility to have children doesn't end in the hospital room when the newborn child emerges. It ends in the hospital room when the soul of the parent departs, leaving behind those who are inspired to continue to build their legacy. Every moment in between is meant to care for, think about, and give to these precious gifts that we were entrusted with.[4]

THE THIRD QUESTION

In describing to us the questions that we will be asked after our time in this world is done and we seek entry into the World to Come, the third question on that list is, "Did you engage in the mitzvah of being fruitful and multiplying?"

Note that the question is phrased, "Did you *engage* in the mitzvah" and not simply "did you fulfill it." This is because, as we said, bringing children into the world isn't the type of mitzvah that we *fulfill* and can now check it off the list of "to-dos" along with eating matzah and paying your taxes. It is meant to be performed by constantly engaging in it, refining our skills, stepping up our game, and settling for nothing short than being awesome at it.

I was once giving a seminar on happiness and shared a list of ten ingredients to happiness (ranging from simply having your physical needs taken care of to lofty goals like discovering your purpose in this

---

3   See *Sefer Hachinuch* #598.
4   See *Igros Moshe, Even Ha'ezer* 5:19,7.

world). I argued that all the ingredients on the list are things that people deeply yearn for in their search for happiness. Raising a child came in at number six, sandwiched right in between finding the love of your life and feeling respected.

The audience seemed to agree with my list of ten. But then a woman raised her hand and went on to take issue with happiness ingredient number six. "I do have kids, but many of my friends do not, and sometimes I feel like they live much happier lives because they are not bogged down by anyone, and they are free to come and go as they please." There was a murmur of agreement in the crowd, but I was not ready to back down just yet.

"How would you explain why so many people yearn for children, and even when they can't naturally have children will go to great extremes to receive treatment so that they can indeed be parents, or they might go ahead and adopt a child?"

Apparently, she was not ready to back down just yet either. She responded, "I believe that many of us only have children because, when we are young, we are told that that is what we are *supposed* to do, and not because we really think about why we are doing it." I looked around the room and was further shocked by how many people were nodding in agreement.

Even as I am writing this, I am still not sure whether I fully believe that they really feel that way at their core. At the same time, I sometimes wonder whether we parents might behave in a way with our children that give off the impression that having them was just the "thing to do" rather than something that we did with a sense of mission. I think that society in general loves their children deeply, but also buys into a Hollywood perspective that believes children bog a person down, deflate the spontaneous and adventurous part of us, and kill our romance. Without a strong sense that every moment that we have with our children is building something that is so much bigger than us, we can fall into this tragic way of thinking.

SOCIETY IN GENERAL LOVES THEIR CHILDREN DEEPLY, BUT ALSO BELIEVES THAT CHILDREN BOG A PERSON DOWN, DEFLATE THE SPONTANEOUS PART OF US, AND KILL OUR ROMANCE.

YOU HAVE MORE CHILDREN THAN YOU THINK

Those who do not have biological children can still shine in this mitz-vah just the same.[5] As we mentioned, this aspect of our life mission is so much bigger than bringing a child into this world. It is the act of giving, loving, and building others, specifically the next generation. This is not something that is limited to a biological parent.

There is a powerful message in the Torah on the words: "This is the lineage of Noah; Noah was a righteous man." The midrash points out that after stating, "This is the lineage of Noah," it does not actually mention the names of his children but declares that he "was a righteous man." They derive from there that "the real progeny of righteous people are their good deeds."

In somewhat of a similar style, the Torah introduces us to "the offspring of Aaron and Moses," the two brothers, and then contin-ues only to list the children of Aaron. This prompts *Rashi* to quote the Talmud, which concludes that "one who teaches Torah to his friend's child is considered as if he fathered him."[6]

Another such lesson can be learned from Abraham, whose very name is a contraction of the words *"av hamon goyim,"* the father of the nations. Because of the kindness of love that he showed everyone, he was considered as a father figure to them. This is em-phasized again when he leaves his hometown of Charan en route to Israel. The Torah says that he came there with all his belongings and "the souls that he created in Charan." The Torah refers to his followers as souls that he made. A true father figure!

Our progeny extends way beyond biological children. It includes all those whom we reach out to and impact with our giving and with our love. For some, it can include their community, including one's friends, neighbors, and even the people that they are connected with through their work. For some, the entire Jewish People are viewed as part of

---

5   See Talmud, *Sanhedrin* 19b.
6   Ibid.

their extended family, and for some, the whole wide world is theirs. We are part of the human race, and we are creatures of God, aren't we? In fact, when commenting on the question "Did you fulfill the mitzvah to be fruitful and multiply," one of the great commentators explains the question as "Did you raise orphans and the needy?"[7]

OUR PROGENY EXTENDS WAY BEYOND BIOLOGICAL CHILDREN. IT INCLUDES ALL THOSE WHOM WE REACH OUT TO AND IMPACT WITH OUR GIVING AND WITH OUR LOVE.

Our Sages in *Ethics of Our Fathers* go so far as to encourage us to make "needy people members of our household." They don't simply say, "Be nice to people." They emphasize that they should be *b'nei beitcha*, literally, "children of your home."

This means that if we were to compare a biological parent of a child who is disengaged and checked out of their child's life with someone who is playing a giving-loving role in someone's life who may not be their blood relative, the latter is actually doing more to accomplish their mission!

HABITS OF LEGACY BUILDERS

PUT THE RIGHT PEOPLE FIRST

It is not uncommon for people to be more motivated to solve problems outside of their immediate circle while neglecting the needs of the ones who need them the most. There are a few reasons for this.

First, it is much more glamorous and exciting to take on a major world challenge than the mundane tasks of dealing with one's family and inner circle. There is no shortage of social media attention for people who rally for social issues or who travel to Africa to help provide clean water. But we don't get as many likes for making our kids their favorite dinner, covering for a coworker who needs our help, or lending an ear for a neighbor who just needs to unload. And often, when we don't get kudos from others, we tend not to give sufficient kudos to ourselves. But when we look at the Torah, we see the opposite message.

---

7   See *Maharasha, Shabbos* loc cit.

Think about Abraham and Sarah, who had spent the majority of their life successfully invested in teaching the world about God. But we only get close and personal with them with the words of the Torah, "*lech lecha*," when the focus of their mission changes. It is then that they are directed to transplant themselves to the Land of Israel, where they will finally merit to have a child, and their family would blossom. Up until that moment, they had only their mission of spreading morality to the masses to focus on. But now their focus would change. It would be about their family.

The story of Isaac and Rebecca mostly revolves around their children—first in praying to have children, and then when they do have their twins, Jacob and Esau, the stories revolve around the relationship that Isaac and Rebecca had with each one of them. In fact, when speaking about the relationship between these parents and their sons, we see for the first time the term "love" mentioned in the context of the parent-child relationship. Outside of their role as parents, we do not hear too much about their other accomplishments. Seemingly, the Torah is emphasizing that the accomplishment of raising and loving one's "children" takes priority even over going out and affecting the masses.

WE ALL WANT TO DO SOMETHING GREAT IN THE WORLD, BUT WE FORGET THAT THE PEOPLE WHO MOST NEED US TO BE GREAT ARE THE PEOPLE CLOSEST TO US.

We all want to do something great in the world, but we forget that the people who most need us to be great are the people closest to us. I have had conversations with people who are deeply searching for ways to grow but refuse to address the rifts and issues that they have with their immediate loved ones.

There are certainly times when we are called upon to do great things, but it is so crucial to keep in mind that you do not have to give away a kidney to accomplish your life's mission. And if you choose to, that is absolutely incredible, but you still have to show up every day for your family and for your loved ones (as soon as you recover, that is).

The story is told of a young married man aspiring for spiritual greatness approaching his rabbi with a complaint. "All I want to do is reach for great spiritual heights through prayer, meditation, and study, but my wife keeps on disturbing me with requests to do mundane chores like doing the dishes and taking out the garbage." The rabbi asked the young married man for a day to think about the solution. The next day, the young man hears a knock on the door of his home. He opens the door and sees none other than his great rabbi standing at his front door. "I thought of a solution to your problem," says the rabbi. "*I will* come and wash your dishes and take out your garbage." The young man understood from the rabbi that true greatness is about taking care of the needs that present themselves right in front of your eyes.

Another reason why people are more likely to show up for people in distant circles at the expense of one's family and friends is because those in our closest circles are the most aware of the flaws in our character, and therefore, we often feel inadequate around them. We lose motivation to be our best selves because we think that they will look at us as a sham since they know our flaws and weaknesses.

Ask a person who is going through struggles with their loved ones to make a list of their very best qualities. In my experience, very often they will answer: "It depends who you ask. The people at work will say that I am a problem solver, relaxed under pressure, pleasant to be around, etc." And then they continue, "But my family probably wouldn't say that about me." What a tragedy! The amazing gifts that make us unique are not shining through for the people who need it the most.

The reason is that so often our confidence has been shattered due to past failures. When we are around them, we think, "I am not really a problem solver, because I couldn't find a solution when they needed me. I am not relaxed under pressure, because look how often I snap at the kids. I am not pleasant to be around, because I feel so grumpy sometimes at home." We write a different script for ourselves when we are around the people who know us best—and it is not at all pretty.

One of the most important aspects of our mission in this world is to take the vision of the person that we know we can be, the image of our best self, and show up consistently in that way for the people that need us most. And when we mess up, because nobody is perfect, we realize that the mess-up is only a temporary setback from us becoming the people that we so badly yearn to be.

I encourage you to try writing down all of your best qualities *when you are at your best.* Then make a list of the ten to fifteen people who are in your immediate circles who need you the most. Include in it your spouse, children, close friends, and parents (especially those with elderly ones). Next to each of their names, write what role you play in their life, what you mean to them, and what you think you should be for them in the ideal relationship. Then consider this: If you would use all of those amazing qualities and channel it toward being the person they need you to be, how would you look? How would you feel about yourself and about them in that scenario?

When we look at the people in our life—family members, neighbors, coworkers—it is essential that we realize that these people are *all* part of our mission. We perfect the element of water by "watering" and giving life to the people who look up to us and who need us most. They did not just randomly end up in our lives. They are part and parcel of what we are here to accomplish. In every interaction that you have with the people that are in your inner circle, it is essential to keep front and center in your mind that they have been placed in your life because there is something about your relationship that is essential to your mission. By investing in them in this way, they will be the ones to carry on our dreams and our values so that even long after we have passed, what we stood for will live on.

summary

We have seen how bringing new life into the world and raising it to carry on your legacy is a key to self-mastery over the water element and a central role in what we are supposed to contribute to the world.

Included in this is

- being mindful that bringing children into the world isn't just about having babies. It is about raising, loving, and nurturing a new life who will carry on your values and add to them with their own individual expression;

- anyone who is dependent on your love and your direction is considered your child;
- keep your children your priority and the more glamorous causes second;
- show up as your best self for the people that you love, and do not get discouraged because you have failed in the past.

11

WATER (PART 3)—
THE POWER OF HOPE

NEFESH LEVEL/ ELEMENT	OBSTACLES	HOW TO ELEVATE	PERSONIFIED BY
Feeling level/ Water	Lust	Channeled pleasure Deep love Hope	Isaac and Rebecca

Every gate has been locked shut
except for the gates of tears.

Talmud, Bava Metzia 59a

PAIN AND HOPE

Why do bad things happen to good people?

This question is at the center of all philosophical and religious discussion and has been for millennia. There is no mystery of life greater than this. It seems that every single person needs to go through some share of pain in this world, some great and some small, as part of their life mission.

A day doesn't go by that we don't hear of people going through challenges ranging from minor inconveniences to very serious financial troubles, health issues, or—God forbid—loss of a loved one. These events seem unfair in our mind. They throw our lives into a loop and make us question ourselves and God. We look for answers and try to understand, but usually come up empty.

ALL OF THE PAIN AND SUFFERING A PERSON GOES THROUGH IN THEIR LIFETIME IS ALSO DIRECTLY CONNECTED TO THEIR MISSION IN THIS WORLD.

We try to console ourselves with clichés and platitudes, such as "Everything happens for a reason"; "What doesn't kill you makes you stronger"; "This, too, is for the good," etc. In many situations, we eventually see how it was, indeed, for the good, or how it did make us stronger, but not always. So often we are just left with the lingering question...why?

All of the pain and suffering a person goes through in their lifetime is also directly connected to their mission in this world, usually in ways that are beyond our understanding.

The element of water and the emotional realm is not only the place within us that we feel pleasure; it is also the place inside of us that we feel pain. These are the bitter waters in our life that feel like they are trying to pull us in and drown us. But it is at this level that another emotion is born that is essential to the perfection of our character: hope.

The waters of hope, like the waters of love, have the power to give life and vitality no matter what we are going through in life. Just as water is a sign of new life and a symbol of renewal, the water element inside of us is what gives us new life even when we feel like everything is crashing down. We find that prayer, which is an expression of hope and yearning, is also symbolized by water in the verse, "I will pour my heart out like water."[1] Tears as well symbolize hope and prayer. This emotion of hope is part of our journey to self-mastery.

THE FOURTH QUESTION

That some degree of adversity and pain is part of our mission in this world is evident from the fourth question that will be asked of us by the Heavenly tribunal: "Did you hope for deliverance (from trouble)?"

---

1   Lamentations 2:19.

Remarkably, one of the main accomplishments that we carry with us to the Next World is how we dealt with suffering when it came our way. Did we let it turn us into bitter and cold people, or did we stay positive? Did we stay hopeful?

Our Sages teach us that no matter how bad it seems, "Even when a sharp sword is resting on your neck, do not withhold yourself from believing in the Almighty's compassion."[2] This means that no matter how bad it seems, things can always change, and even when something terrible has happened, and we feel like we will never be able to recover—we doubt whether we can go on living because the pain is so, so deep—do not stop believing that the Almighty will help you heal and give you the strength to go on.

Once again, we turn to Isaac and Rebecca, who embody this trait and are the archetypes for hope even when all seems lost.

Isaac himself is a child of parents who were unable to have children. Then, the ordeal of the "binding of Isaac" was another moment when it seemed that all was lost. Similar to the time of the Great Flood, when Isaac is bound and on the verge of being sacrificed, it seems that God's attribute of judgment and discipline has overpowered His compassion. And it seems that the legacy of Abraham would never come to fruition. And then, all of a sudden, everything changes. There is a great revelation; Isaac will not be sacrificed, and new potential is born! This moment of salvation is one that we invoke in our prayers whenever we are praying for redemption.

Isaac is a man of hope and prayer. When Rebecca first meets him, he is out in the field, meditating and praying. When the couple is not able to have children, the Torah says that they sat and prayed until they were answered. They are a symbol of hope.[3] Our Sages

---

2   Talmud, *Berachos* 10a.

3   See note 1 on p. 95. The second blessing of the *Amidah* references Isaac. It is in this blessing that we acknowledge the gift of rain, the element of water, and giving of life, and it is in this blessing that the concept of deliverance is mentioned: "You support the fallen and You heal

teach us further that it was in the merit of Isaac's prayers in Heaven that the Jewish People were redeemed from Egypt.[4]

The very name Isaac means "he will rejoice." This term of rejoicing is specifically a joy that is born when one is going through a difficult, even life-threatening time, and makes it through. In Hebrew, the name is pronounced *Yitzchak*, and the Hebrew letters (*yud, tzaddi, ches, kuf*) are the very same letters that make up the Hebrew words *keitz chai*, the end of life. And yet, with a little shuffling of the letters, i.e., a slightly different perspective, it becomes a word that means rejoicing!

THE CAUSE OF SUFFERING

Let's take a deeper look into the role of adversity and pain in one's life to understand the role that it plays in our mission. It is important to remember that there are really no words or philosophies that can fully ease the pain of someone who is going through such difficulties in their lifetime. However, a little more of an understanding about what is behind pain and suffering might at least add a little bit of light.

Our Sages teach us that there are two categories of suffering that we endure in this lifetime:[5]

1. The first is suffering that is meant to be a wake-up call for us that we need to be growing.
2. The second is called "suffering [that comes] from [God's] love," and the reason for it is beyond our comprehension.

---

the sick; You free the captives and preserve Your faith with those asleep in the dust. Who is like You, Master of mighty deeds? Who can be compared to You, O King Who causes death and restores life, and causes Your salvation to sprout?"

4   The name Isaac's numerical value is 208. This is the same numerical value as the word "*va'eira*," which is the Torah portion in which the redemption from Egypt began. The midrash (quoted by the commentary of the *Rosh* in *Parashas Shemos*) says that it was in the merit of Isaac that the Jewish People were redeemed from Egypt because he petitioned God for their early release. The Talmud (*Shabbos* 89b) says that it is the merit of Isaac that will bring the final redemption.

5   Talmud, *Berachos* 5a.

Let's look at each one.

The first category of suffering is meant to be a wake-up call to change. Sometimes, God might throw at us a bit of a curve-ball in our life for the sake of shaking us up to let us know that we made

WHEN EVERYTHING IS GOING SMOOTH, IT IS EASY TO BECOME COMPLACENT WITH WHO WE ARE AND WHAT WE HAVE ACCOMPLISHED.

a wrong turn someplace along the way, or that we should be doing more. When everything is going smooth, it is easy to become complacent with who we are and what we have accomplished. Suffering can be a nudge to make us stop and think and ask ourselves what the message is.

Therefore, we should first take a look at areas of our life where we might not be living up to our full potential. Are we hurting people? Have we been fully honest? If we see no obvious place where we are falling short in our character, we are encouraged to take something on spiritually.

Along these lines, as difficult as this might be to accept, we might find that the suffering itself can actually bring out some of the beautiful aspects of our personality.

1. First, pain *deflates* our ego and allows us to make space for God. When things run smoothly, we tend to stop thinking about God, and our level of belief in ourselves inflates. We communicate less with God and start believing that we can handle anything that comes our way. As our ego *inflates*, other character flaws begin to surface. But when we go through any kind of suffering, we realize how dependent we are on God. We begin to speak to God and are humbled by the experience. Eventually, we see that our other character flaws also begin to fade away, and we are able to access a new inner beauty.

2. Second, it sensitizes us to the needs of others. Without any pain in our life, it is difficult to relate to the pain of others. Though we might try to intellectually relate to what someone might be going through, those thoughts cannot fully penetrate our hearts. When we go through pain, we become more sensitive and compassionate to other people's pain.

3. Third, it causes us to pray. The prayers and the tears of someone who is going through suffering are the most powerful prayers. Though we might not see how those prayers are working toward the outcome that we were hoping for, Judaism teaches that they might have a deep effect on the world in a much bigger way than we will ever know in this lifetime.

Our Sages teach us that every single word of prayer that we utter has an effect on this world. The Talmud teaches us that the reason that our matriarchs were barren at first was because through their prayers for children, they spiritually built the foundations for all of the Jewish nation.

SUFFERING OF LOVE

The second category of suffering is what is referred to as suffering that comes from love. How are we to understand this? If it hurts so much, how can we accept that this is coming from God's love?

To fully embrace this aspect of suffering, we need to internalize a deep truth about who and what we really are: *neshamos*, spiritual souls, sparks of Godliness embodied in this lifetime on a temporary journey that is part of a much bigger picture that we do not fully understand.

For some souls, that journey is meant to be eighty or ninety years. And for some, their mission can be to come to this planet for a very short time—a week, a year, a few years—and then be taken away from the world. For this pure soul, this short time in this world might be all it needs to accomplish its mission. For the others that are affected by the loss, the pain and suffering is tremendous. This, too, relates to their own mission and what they need to accomplish.

Some souls are given a body that is healthy and active with much to accomplish. Other souls are given bodies that are disabled, but have the powerful ability to open the hearts of the people who care for them and pray for them in a very unique way. Some souls are given a mission that will involve tears of joy, and others tears of pain. Who knows, though, which river of tears penetrates deeper in the cosmic masterplan?

We mentioned earlier that Jewish tradition teaches that every single one of our souls was created in the beginning of time and was present in Adam and Eve in the Garden of Eden. When Adam and Eve fell from their blissful state, the collective soul of humanity was harmed, and this whole adventure that we are on is coming to restore humanity to its original greatness.

Pieces of that collective soul enter into the world again and again throughout history and make their home in different hosts. Every individual that comes into this world adds more and more merit to the soul that they possess, bringing it even closer to its true greatness. We might not experience that greatness here in the consciousness that we experience in this lifetime, but the journey is bigger than just this lifetime.

Where a soul is coming from in this long journey will define what challenges it will have to confront in this lifetime, and what hurdles it will have to overcome. Will it be here for a short time or a long time? What will its struggles be like? Will they be spiritual, emotional, or physical? What kind of people will it come into contact with in this world?

Judaism teaches that after this lifetime is over, the soul ultimately returns to its source, where it experiences the pleasure of true and pure consciousness. In that World of Truth, we will fully understand how the ups and downs in this lifetime contributed to our journey, and how it was part of a master plan that ultimately led to a better us and a better world, even though we could not understand it at the time.

And, while we can only imagine that ethereal destination as nothing but a dream, it is in fact a deeper reality than we experience in our time on this earth. Just as when a person is experiencing a dream while they are sleeping, it seems absolutely real at the time, but upon waking up, we realize that it was just a dream. During our lifetime, as well, our consciousness leads us to believe that there can be no stronger reality than this, but that, too, is an illusion. It is only based on our frame of reference. We are here, so this must be the greatest reality there is. Jewish teaching believes that that is incorrect.

With this in mind, we can understand what the Talmud means by pain of love. This painful experience that we are going through is not coming from a place of harshness or discipline; on the contrary, it is elevating our soul in ways that are much deeper than we can grasp. For souls whose mission might seem harsh in this world, those unique individuals are the pipelines for Divine love and compassion to flow into the world in abundance.

HABITS OF HOPEFUL PEOPLE—VISUALIZE BETTER TIMES

We mentioned above that we are asked the question: "Did you hope for deliverance?" The actual Hebrew word for hope that is used is *tzipisa*, which can alternatively be translated as "envision." This translation calls our attention to a principle that we mentioned above, when we spoke about the abundance mindset and the power of *emunah*. And that is as follows: What you believe will affect the reality. It is built into the power of our minds. The most effective way to cause yourself to believe something is to envision it happening.

No matter what you are going through, envision the outcome turning out to be the best possible scenario. Envision how this can actually be good for you. Envision that this pain is actually making you a stronger, better, and more powerful person—not to mention what it must be doing for your soul!

Imagine all pain in this world like the pain of childbirth. Though the birth pangs are one of the most intense pains the human body will experience, the mother believes that each contraction is bringing the baby one step closer to taking his or her first breath. Though it feels like death, it is actually the beginning of life. And at any moment, that next strong contraction might be the one that will push the baby to the point of emerging in the light of the world.

This pain that you are going through might be the contraction that will push you into the next stage of your life, which will be full of peace and joy!

summary

We have seen how staying hopeful through suffering is a key to self-mastery over the water element and is a core part of our emotional realm that we are supposed to develop in this lifetime. Included in this is

- never giving up hope or allowing yourself to turn bitter, no matter how bad things seem to be;

- praying for deliverance;
- introspection as to what God might be trying to tell you and how this suffering might be making you a better person;
- being mindful that some suffering is "suffering of love," which is somehow connected to our souls;
- visualizing what a positive outcome or a better future will look like.

12
WIND (PART 1)—
SEARCHING FOR TRUTH

NEFESH LEVEL/ ELEMENT	OBSTACLES	HOW TO ELEVATE	PERSONIFIED BY
Intellectual level/Wind	Wasting time False beliefs Idle chatter	Intellectual honesty Pursuit of truth Meaningful communication	Jacob Rachel and Leah

The seal of God is truth.

Shabbat 55a

EXAMINING LIFE

"The unexamined life is not worth living." This idea, and the movement it represented, resulted in the death sentence of the Greek philosopher, Socrates, in the 5th century BCE. He was charged with corrupting the youth by getting them to challenge the norm and think for themselves. But the story of a man being sentenced to death because he challenged the world to think for themselves goes back much farther.

A millennium earlier, the patriarch Abraham, whom we spoke about earlier, had to flee his homeland because of a death sentence put on him for the very same reason. He looked around at the world that he was born into and realized it made no sense. He questioned and questioned and came up with vastly different conclusions about God, the universe, and morality than what was commonly accepted at that time. Rather than keeping it to himself, he began to engage with the locals until he amassed a following of tens of thousands of devoted students.

It is for this reason that he is referred to as a "Hebrew," which comes from the word *Ivri*, the one who stands on the "other side of the river." He was unashamed to challenge what all others take for granted. A true free-thinker. This process that began with Abraham was brought to an even greater degree with his grandson Jacob, who would become known as "the man of truth."

This brings us to the next step in fulfilling our mission: an endless pursuit of the truth. Throughout our life, we are meant to constantly upgrade, deepen, and refine our beliefs about what is true and what is false, our perspectives about what is good and what is bad, and what we consider right and wrong.

This process of learning how to think independently in one's search for truth is connected to the inner element of wind, the intellectual level of our inner world. Wind creates movement just as the intellect has the power to create change in a person. The movement of wind also represents the constant movement of our thoughts and development of ideas, as a person needs to be open to analyzing their beliefs again and again. Wind also represents speech, which is the external manifestation of our intellect, as the process of searching for clarity requires asking questions and engaging in dialogue with other people that we can learn from.

There are many aspects of our belief system that constantly require upgrading. Included in this is

- how we understand God and our relationship with the Divine;
- how we determine our values and set goals;
- what causes and rights we believe are worth fighting for;
- how we invest our time, energy, and resources;
- what we are living for and whom we are meant to be.

Human beings are at a disadvantage. By the time we are mature enough and our brains developed enough to really think independently, we have already been "indoctrinated" with beliefs about how things "should be" and "have to be," about who we are "supposed to be" and "need to be." To look at the world with fresh eyes requires us to push back on those limiting beliefs and think fresh about who we are and what our world can look like. This is a process that does not come naturally.

BY THE TIME WE ARE MATURE ENOUGH TO REALLY THINK INDEPENDENTLY, WE HAVE ALREADY BEEN "INDOCTRINATED" WITH BELIEFS ABOUT HOW THINGS "SHOULD BE."

Part of your mission is to question everything around you. Know why you are living the life that you are living. Clarify your beliefs and your identity. Explore your roots. How do your beliefs line up with those of your parents and grandparents? What beliefs do you carry with you that are nothing more than ideas that you digested before you were mature enough to really process them? And if you come up with your own individual perspectives, are you brave enough to pursue them? And are you ready to pursue a life of individuality?

This requires immersing oneself in constant mind expansion and intellectual pursuits that deeply matter, gaining a deeper understanding of the world and humanity for the sake of making the world a better place. It involves developing one's brain to think clearly and ethically through more and more learning, combined with inner analysis and outer dialogue with peers, with those who know more than us, and with those who disagree with us.

JACOB—MAN OF ETHICAL DILEMMAS

The relentless search for truth is the subject of the next section of the Book of Genesis and is embodied in the third of our Patriarchs, Jacob, referred to in Rabbinic tradition as a man of truth, based on the verse, "You give truth to Jacob."[1] Jacob is perhaps the most nuanced personality in all of Torah, and therefore his story must be understood well.

---

1   Micah 7:20.

A superficial "Sunday-school-type" understanding of Jacob might lead one to wonder whether Jacob was a sly and sneaky person who tricks his brother (to acquire the rights to the firstborn) and his father (to steal away the blessings). Indeed, many are guilty of falling into that trap. A deeper study of Jacob unlocks a much more sophisticated understanding of both his life, as well as the meaning of truth.

> Torah describes Jacob in his early years as "a man of wholesomeness, dwelling in tents."[2] Throughout the Torah, the term "tent" is used as a reference to deep Torah study.
>
> It was his deep commitment and understanding of the Torah's truth that Jacob amasses in his youth that allows him to navigate the complications and ethical dilemmas of dealing with many complicated and threatening situations that he faces throughout his lifetime. His sharpness and ability to appropriately read and respond to each situation protects him from encounters with those who are trying to harm him, and sets him up to fulfill his mission to become the progenitor of the Jewish nation.

The search for truth doesn't typically present us with choices that are black and white. On the contrary, most difficult moral decisions that we must make require us to pin certain values against others. We want to do what is right but are confused by the various different factors that come in to play and complicate things. On top of that, we are usually heavily pressured to satisfy others or to go along with what is popular opinion, even if popular opinion might be motivated by factors other than just what is right and true. The story of Jacob shows us firsthand that sometimes what seems wrong on the outside is actually the correct stand to take.

MOST DIFFICULT MORAL DECISIONS THAT WE MUST MAKE REQUIRE US TO PIN CERTAIN VALUES AGAINST OTHERS.

2   Genesis 25:27.

A seminal moment in the life of Jacob involved this particularly complicated scenario:

His father, Isaac, blind and approaching death, requests of his other son Esau to bring him food and to receive the blessings of the birthright, a privilege that would be awarded to him as the firstborn son. Isaac is unaware that the rights to the firstborn privileges had actually been discarded by Esau many years ago and purchased from him by Jacob. Aware of what is about to go down, Isaac's wife, Rebecca, requests of Jacob to disguise himself as Esau and fool the blind Isaac into giving him the blessings. When Jacob approaches his father in disguise, his father asks who it is that is standing before him. Jacob responds, "It is I, Esau, your firstborn."

On the surface this seems to be a lie, which is particularly surprising coming from the specific individual whom the Torah calls the man of truth. But Jacob did have a rightful claim to the blessings after purchasing the right of firstborn from Esau. Jacob, and his mother Rebecca, understood that Isaac was blinded to the wayward path that Esau took, and rather than causing him the pain of revealing Esau's flaws, they chose to try to take the blessings in a more concealed way.

But Isaac is surprisingly more aware than expected, as is evident from his response: "The voice is the voice of Jacob, and the hands are the hands of Esau." He then goes ahead and blesses him. Why would Isaac give the blessing to this seeming imposter? Doesn't the voice give away that the one standing before him is not the one whom the blessing was intended for?

The answer is that even in this moment of confusion, there is one aspect of clarity: the voice is the voice of Jacob. Isaac knows that voice. It the voice of honesty and truth. The voice of someone who is rooted deeply in Torah values and would not violate that unless he has analyzed the situation and has established what is the correct mode of action. Isaac places his trust in the voice of Jacob, the voice of truth.

The struggle between conflicting values is not uncommon for one who is on a path of growth and searching for truth. The truth-seeker often finds himself embracing values that are not popular with family and friends or that go against the trending values of society.

THE TRUTH-SEEKER OFTEN FINDS HIMSELF EMBRACING VALUES THAT ARE NOT POPULAR WITH FAMILY AND FRIENDS OR THAT GO AGAINST THE TRENDING VALUES OF SOCIETY.

This is especially true when one is trying to embrace a spiritual or religious path. As one goes down this path, they find that not only are their family and friends not receptive but often quick to vilify the one who is trying to grow. I often deal with students who are facing extreme resistance from their parents, siblings, or even children, who will do everything to stand in the way of the spiritual growth of their loved one.

Western society also makes it increasingly difficult to engage in any sort of dialogue involving certain hot-button topics. Conversations that could be rich and respectful often turn into nasty name-calling and labeling. People are no longer free to express their opinions without the fear of setting off a nuclear explosion.

The Torah specifically presents Jacob as this nuanced personality to teach us that not all truth is as simple as a slogan or hashtag, but needs to be fully explored at every angle.

INTEGRITY

Our intellectual integrity and its similarity to wind also brings up a challenge. Just as one can let go of a false belief in the pursuit of truth, so too, we become vulnerable to letting go of truth when we are influenced or pressured to take a new position. We also need to be careful not to fall into the trap of groupthink, going along with what everyone else believes without giving it the proper analysis.

We once again return to our Patriarch Jacob and his wives, Rachel and Leah, who embody the ability to exist in an immoral environment for so many years, yet remain true to the highest standards and morals.

After fleeing from Esau, who was trying to kill him, Jacob goes to the house of his uncle, Lavan, to find a wife. The holy matriarchs Rachel and Leah, both of whom are destined to marry Jacob, both grew up in a house full of paganism and dishonesty, yet on their own they developed into righteous, holy women who would become the matriarchs of the Jewish nation.

Jacob spends the next twenty years in his home, during which he builds a family of righteous children. He works for Lavan, who is the last guy on earth that you would want as your boss. He is greedy, dishonest, and looking to take advantage. In an environment like that, one would imagine that Jacob would have somehow fallen from his high level of spirituality or at least his standard of honesty. Yet, Jacob reaffirms his trustworthiness later on in his dramatic final speech to his father-in-law: "I was [in the field] by day when the heat consumed me, and the frost at night, and my sleep wandered from my eyes."[3]

On the return back to his homeland, Jacob's commitment to the truth is confirmed once again in one final seminal moment. He encounters a seemingly hostile angel and, after an all-night wrestling match, emerges victorious. He then asks the angel to bless him. Instead, the angel gives him an additional name, Yisrael, or Israel. This name would become the identity of his family and the nation that would come from him, the children of Israel.

The name Yisrael contains in it many meanings, but one of the most powerful interpretations is a secret that is hidden amongst the letters of the word. The name *Yisrael* (spelled *yud, shin, reish, alef, lamed*) contains the very letters that would spell a different phrase: *rosh li*, my head (i.e., my intellect) belongs to me.

What an appropriate name for Jacob, one who has immersed himself in analytical thought and who understands how to maintain his identity in any situation and despite any negative influence. My head is mine! You cannot sway me through pressure or through groupthink. I own my beliefs.

---

3   Genesis 31:40.

HABITS OF TRUTH SEEKERS

Because of the challenge of conflicting values and our ability to easily be influenced, how do we go about the process of truth-seeking and establishing our beliefs and values? How do we know if all values are just relative to the time, the society, and the trends, or if there are certain absolutes? And where do we turn to learn the methodology that we can apply when we are faced with such dilemmas?

Jacob was the man of truth because he sat in the tents of Torah study. The Torah is the blueprint for ethical living—the guidebook that the Creator of the world gave to guide us on this path. It is more than just a guide to Judaism or an inspiring book of how to live a better life. It is actually a direct path to experiencing God by fusing together one's own mind and the Divine intellect.

In the words of the great Rabbi Moshe Chaim Luzzato in *The Way of God*, where he speaks about the Godly influence that can be found in Torah study:

> For behold, the Master of the world put together a compilation of words and statements that constitute all of the five books of the Torah, and after them the Prophets and Writings. And He bound His Divine energy in such a way that when these statements would be spoken, this energy would be brought down for the one speaking them.

Therefore, part of accomplishing our mission in this lifetime will involve us delving into the Torah and becoming as proficient in its study as possible.

We mentioned earlier one of the questions that we are asked by the Heavenly tribunal upon our arrival at the gates of the World to Come: "Did you set daily routines for your Torah?" We pointed out that the question focuses not just on whether we studied Torah but on whether we made it a habit.

One of the major barriers to daily study is lack of time. The work/life balance is already demanding, and the idea of taking out a significant amount of time each day to study seems overwhelming. But for the vast majority of people who do not dedicate time for their growth, it falls by the wayside.

Any new habit that we are serious about forming will likely not be accomplished unless we institute the practice of time-blocking. Time-blocking means, as it sounds, to set aside a block of time on one's calendar to do activities that would not necessarily make it into the calendar because it is not a meeting or an appointment. Because many of the tasks that are crucial to long-term success are not necessarily the most pressing, it is likely that these things will be neglected if they are not put into the calendar and treated with the same respect as an appointment with a client. When you time-block for a specific task, you are telling yourself that this is something that is as important as anything else on the calendar.

And while it seems overwhelming to block out daily time for Torah study, consider this. Research has shown that one of the most common habits of the most successful and wealthiest people in the world is that they time-block large chunks of time every day to learn something new. They do this by reading, taking courses, or listening to podcasts. It is not unheard of for CEOs of major companies to read 3–5 hours a day! This is because they understand that expanding their mind is crucial to their success.

If the busiest people can see the great value in expanding their mind, certainly engaging in an activity that not only expands the mind but awakens the soul is worthy of time-blocking significant chunks of time. And, indeed, we can attest to the fact that those who understand this have figured out a way to make it happen. This is usually done by incorporating it into their morning or evening routines.

In Jewish life, blocking out time every day to study Torah is part and parcel of the life of even the busiest people. Many have made it the practice to wake up earlier to study Torah, while others have used their commuting time to consume all sorts of Torah media. The NYC subway is full of commuters with books in their hands or audio in their ears, as they use their transit time to consume knowledge that will expand their mind and their souls by utilizing the thousands of resources that make Torah study easily and conveniently accessible for the masses.

WHAT AREA OF TORAH SHOULD A PERSON STUDY?

Throughout this book, we have seen how the Written Torah, which is how we refer to the five books of the Torah, is the blueprint of creation. All other areas of Torah study are branching off of this Divine foundation. Each area of study opens up new fascinating worlds in the exploration of this Divine wisdom, taking us in many diverse directions but always leading back home to the source, i.e., the five books. There is something in the Torah that can spark the excitement of anyone, and depending on one's personality and brain type, different people will find different parts of Torah exciting. But no matter how different the learning styles are of different people, all Torah explorers are in a sense united in that they are all exploring the same wisdom but are just looking at it from different angles.

But precisely because there are so many different paths to take, knowing where to invest oneself is often complicated and overwhelming. Often, a person must try many different areas of study before they find the path that is right for them. The important thing is to stay committed even when it seems like one has hit a dead end. It is just a matter of time until he will find the right path for him. It is for this reason that we actually include in part of every prayer for help "to find our portion of the Torah."

Typically, the area of Torah study that one will feel connected to will be somewhat connected to how you are wired in other areas in their life. Are you more of an "intellectual" who might be pulled toward study of Talmud (to be discussed more in the next chapter), or are you more spiritual and might therefore take more interest in learning about Jewish prayer and the deeper meaning of mitzvot? Do you enjoy more of the practical aspects of Jewish law or the abstract thinking of Jewish philosophy? Are you more inspired by learning an ancient text with commentaries or a contemporary thinker?

These questions are just scratching the surface of the many different paths of Torah that one could take. Every individual must look for guidance from someone who is knowledgeable in the many areas of Torah as well as someone who knows you and can guide you on a path that will be inspiring for you. You must also look inward and discover how you were specifically meant to connect. Find others whom you can share that journey with and mentors who can lead you and guide you further down that path.

summary

We have seen how relentlessly searching for the truth and refining your perspectives are the keys to self-mastery over the wind element and the intellectual realm of our *nefesh*.

Included in this is

- constantly questioning, reassessing, and updating your beliefs and convictions;
- seeing "truth" not as a black-and-white objective reality but as the ability to understand the nuances of each situation and to act in the most appropriate way;
- being mindful of the ethical dilemmas that present themselves to us and carefully weighing the different sides;
- time-blocking for daily Torah study, which feeds not only the mind but connects the soul to the Divine energy.

13

WIND (PART 2)— BECOMING A LIFELONG LEARNER

NEFESH LEVEL/ ELEMENT	OBSTACLES	HOW TO ELEVATE	PERSONIFIED BY
Intellectual level/Wind	Wasting time False beliefs Idle chatter	Intellectual honesty Pursuit of truth Meaningful communication	Jacob Rachel and Leah

God grants wisdom; from his mouth comes knowledge and understanding.

Proverbs 2:6

PURSUIT OF WISDOM—THE NEXT QUESTION

One of the first blessings that we make every day, and throughout the day, is acknowledging that God "formed man with wisdom." This mention of Divine wisdom refers to the tool that God used to create man as well as the inner drive and built-in potential of all human beings to discover the vast amounts of brilliant wisdom that exists in creation. In the previous chapter, we showed how truth-seeking through constant

124

questioning and reassessing one's beliefs leads to mastery over the inner element of wind and the intellectual level of our *nefesh* life-force. In this chapter, we delve a little deeper into the habits and the processes of those who are constantly looking to expand their mind through their pursuit of wisdom and become lifelong learners.

The important role of becoming a lifelong learner as part of our life mission is evident in that it can be found in the next question that is on our Sage's list of what will be asked of us by the Heavenly tribunal in our post-life interview, as our soul stands at the gate of the World to Come:

"Did you engage in deep discussions of wisdom?" and "Did you understand one matter from another (i.e., did you seek to fully explore the depth of that wisdom)?"

The question is not simply asking us whether we read a lot of books or attended many seminars. The Hebrew term for "deep discussions" in this question is *pilpul*. *Pilpul* is defined (by Websters) as "penetrating investigation, disputation, and drawing of conclusions, especially in Talmudic study."[1]

For those readers who might not be familiar with Talmud study, allow me to share with you a glimpse. The process of Talmud study involves analyzing the very minutia of various legal cases and ethical dilemmas, some deliberately far-fetched to fully explore the extremes, and dissecting the language of the Torah and the Rabbinic Sages. In the world of the yeshiva, where Talmud is studied, one finds students involved in the dynamic sharing and intense debating of ideas. It isn't uncommon to find two study partners in such a heated debate with one another to the point that one might fear an all-out brawl! But the moment they step away from their studies, they are even closer friends than before, having fused together spiritually by the common love of Torah and pursuit of what is true.

The goal of this in-depth study is to ingrain in the mind of the students that life is a constant search for truth, and to impress upon them that the process of finding truth requires both in-depth analysis

---

1   Websters Revised Unabridged Dictionary (C & G Merriam, Co., 1913).

of ideas and situations as well as a dynamic give-and-take of differing opinions and conflicting viewpoints. Nothing should be accepted as is, and nothing is black-and-white. A question posed to a Talmudic student is typically not answered with a yes or a no, rather, "It depends," or, "There is a debate about this." And that is just when you ask them what is for lunch!

As we see from the fact that we are asked about it in the afterlife, this dynamic give-and-take isn't just an exercise for yeshiva students; it is a necessary step for us to get to truth and clarity in our own life, and it is therefore central to our mission in this world. Even outside of actual Talmud study, all the ideas we accept as truth that become the guiding principles of our life should undergo this very same rigorous process.

THE TOWER OF BABEL VS. JACOB'S LADDER

We saw earlier that the power to communicate is directly connected to the intellect. Therefore, it is through dialect and meaningful communication that we open up new channels of understanding and clarity while shallow conversation blurs our thinking and creates more confusion, murkiness, and even corruption, as we saw earlier with the generation of the Tower of Babel.

Let's briefly revisit that story and see how, in fact, engaging in deep and meaningful discussion is actually the reparation to crooked thinking and misused conversation of that sinful generation:

> The generation of the Tower of Babylon was comprised of brilliant architects who chose to use their intellect and power of communication to wage a war against spirituality, rather than access it. They were the progenitors of crooked thinking, and their conversations are considered no more than idle chatter. They are remembered by the fact that the word for silly childish talk is referred to as "babble"!
>
> The goal of the generation was to "build a city and a tower with its head in the sky," i.e., to wage war against God.[2] The term "head in

---

2   Genesis 11:4.

the sky" is symbolic of the corruption of their brilliance and power of intellect. This is in contrast to a defining moment in the life of Jacob, the prototype of honest thinking, who dreamed of a ladder "with its feet on the ground and its head reaching to the sky."[3] The addition of the "feet on the ground" shows that Jacob's thought process was logical and "well-grounded," and the addition of the phrase "reaching to (the sky)" shows that it reached its destination of grasping the highest and holiest levels of knowledge.

Furthermore, the story of the Tower and Babel resulted in God "scatter[ing] them over the face of the whole earth" (reminiscent of the phrase "scatter-brained").[4] In direct contrast to this, the story of Jacob's ladder continues with the message that was relayed to Jacob in that prophetic vision—that his children would be "spread out to the west and to the east, to the north and to the south. All the families of the earth shall bless themselves by you and your descendants."

A powerful message emerges from here. Every culture and every society will have its set of beliefs and values that is communicated to the masses and is often blindly accepted as truth. Those beliefs are fleeting as the wind; eventually they are "scattered," and a new set of beliefs and values take over. It is only the beliefs that have their feet on the ground in the form of an unchanging, credible source that will withstand the test of time.

In an incredible twist of fate that can only be attributed to the Divine Hand Who charts the course of history, the area of Torah study that we referred to earlier, that fully engages the intellect through analysis and dialogue to establish unchanging truths, i.e., the Talmud, was actually compiled and perfected in Babylon, the very location where crooked thinking was introduced to the world. Talk about coming full circle!

---

3   Ibid. 28:12.
4   Ibid. 11:9.

HABITS OF LIFELONG LEARNERS

MASTERING THE TWO-STEP THINKING PROCESS

In that final interview, we are asked whether we engaged in deep discussion of "wisdom" and "understanding" one matter from another. The Hebrew word for wisdom is *chochmah*, and the word for understanding is *binah*. These two mental faculties need to be understood as an essential two-step process in our processing of information.

Step #1—Chochmah, Wisdom

Our Sages teach: "Who is considered a *chacham* (wise person)? Someone who learns from everyone." The image that is being painted for us is of a person who is always searching, always curious, always open to learn something new. A lifelong learner whose greatest joy in life is the ability to learn something new. This person is open to the many ideas that will develop through their learning and the many opportunities for inspiration that avail themselves.

Chochmah is the starting point of all learning and thinking because it refers to the information and ideas that originate outside of ourselves. Whenever we learn something new, we are being exposed to information that exists outside of ourselves. The source of this information might be a book, a teacher, or even a hands-on experience, but it is entering into our minds from a source outside of ourselves. But even spending one's life learning and collecting wisdom and learning experiences does not necessarily create a truly enlightened human being. As we are very familiar, our minds can only process so much. We don't fully understand every piece of information, and even what we do, we don't always remember it.

Step #2—Binah, Understanding

The next step in the process is called *binah*. It is here that our mind goes through the stage of processing and analyzing in order to decide what information it really wants to take ownership over. This means that one spends time contemplating what he or she had learned, asking what it means for their life, and how it should affect their lifestyle.

We have all experienced the concept of selective memory—remembering only certain things that we value while forgetting others. The reason this happens is because if we would fully process all of the information that comes our way, our brains would be overwhelmed by all of the information that comes in. It would be more than we can handle and would drain our energy. So, we automatically select what information we want to give more weight and permanence to.

We live in the information age, in which we have access to almost all knowledge available with just a few clicks of a button and for free. There is an overwhelming amount of *chochmah* that we have access to. But having more knowledge at our fingertips can have its downside as well. Since we are constantly accumulating more knowledge, we might not necessarily be fully digesting the knowledge as it comes in before we move on to the next thing.

Without fully processing the ideas that we learn and thinking about what that means to us, we end up with a lot of information but a connection to it that can be very superficial. This is especially problematic when it comes to information that could really make a major impact on one's life if they were to really spend the time contemplating it. So, the *chochmah-binah* partnership in the learning process is about collecting ideas, processing them, and filing them in a way that the information can be accessed and applied.

WITHOUT FULLY PROCESSING THE IDEAS THAT WE LEARN, WE END UP WITH A LOT OF INFORMATION BUT A CONNECTION TO IT THAT CAN BE VERY SUPERFICIAL.

TAPPING INTO YOUR CREATIVE POTENTIAL

The *chochmah-binah* dynamic plays an important role not only in the realm of processing information but also when coming up with ideas, being creative, and in moments of inspiration. All of those things seem to hit us out of the blue. They likely originate somewhere in the brain, even though they feel as if they are somehow being dropped in from elsewhere. When we have an "aha" or a "eureka" moment, it almost feels as if we have had a mini-prophetic revelation. You will consistently hear writers and musicians speak about how their ideas "came to them" or "came through them." This is also referred to as *chochmah*, as the verse states: "and *chochmah* emerges from nothingness."[5] Just like in the learning process, *chochmah* is coming from an outside source, so too, in the formation of an idea, there seems to be this mysterious outside source that dropped it into our brains.

But an idea that drops in is also in danger of remaining in the realm of the abstract if it is not fleshed out using the power of *binah*. Until it is articulated with words, written down on a piece of paper, played on an instrument, or sketched out on a paper, it is in danger of evaporating as quickly as it materializes.

Often, my children will tell me during a conversation, "I know what I am trying to say, I am just having a hard time saying it." To which I respond, "That means that you are probably saying something very deep, and the idea just needs a little more time to bake. So, take your time and let the idea take hold." This is the process of *binah* taking place.

In the realm of motivation, we see the *chochmah-binah* dynamic once again. Motivation is often triggered by something outside of ourselves. Maybe we are in the presence of someone very inspiring, or we hear a fiery pep talk, or experience a powerful moment, and suddenly we feel the vibrations of our inner will becoming awakened inside of us. At that moment, we see our life with clarity; we know where we need to go. Our Sages note that the word *chochmah* can be broken down into two words: *koach*, which means "potential," and *mah*, which means "what." Thus, *chochmah* means "the potential of what can be."

But like a flash of lightning, it illuminates, and then it disappears. All that is left is for us to take that moment and turn it into a concrete plan while we still feel some of the aftershocks and before it completely fades away.

Information that isn't processed, ideas that are never developed, and inspiration that doesn't result in a plan are all examples of *chochmah* without *binah*. And they are all great tragedies.

This means that when you have an "aha" moment or a moment of inspiration, you don't just let it fade away. You determine how to act on

5   Job 28:12.

it and how to turn it into a plan for action. It is only at the level of *binah* that all of the information that you received through your learning, thinking, and inspiration synchronizes and creates an original piece of inner artwork that is authentically yours.

MEANINGFUL CONVERSATIONS

The *binah* process is both an internal process and also one that should be done with others through articulation, listening, and debating, as we mentioned before regarding the study of Talmud. This is why the wind element is the root of both the intellect as well as the ability to communicate. Speech is in fact nothing more than the wind that flows from inside of us in the form of our voice. It is no wonder, then, that Jacob, the Torah's symbol of constant learning and intellectual honesty, is identified by his voice, as the verse says: "The voice is the voice of Jacob." Surely, this is not a reference to the tone of his vocal cords! It is a reference to the content that comes out of his mouth. His intellectual honesty is manifest through his voice of truth.

In contrast to the idle chatter of the generation of Babel, the voice of Jacob is developed through meaningful discussion and rich conversations. The saying goes: "Great people discuss ideas. Average people discuss events. Small people discuss other people." Which category do you fall into? Let's expound.

Great people look for meaningful conversations. They view their conversations as an opportunity to learn something new, to solve a problem, to get inspired, or create a deeper connection with the person they are speaking with. They use small talk only as a springboard to get to those deeper conversations, where they can discuss things that are more meaningful and valuable.

GREAT PEOPLE LOOK FOR MEANINGFUL CONVERSATIONS.

Average people look for conversations on things that interest them. Perhaps it is the news, politics, sports, or pop culture. Their conversations often revolve around the events that are going on in their lives (irrespective of whether those events are particularly significant or not.) Much of these conversations fall into a category that we would call "small talk."

The lowest level of conversation is focused on other people. This is the default conversation for those who have nothing else to speak about. Obviously, if that talk about other people is negative, that conversation falls into a category called *lashon hara*, gossip, which Jewish tradition considers one of the gravest transgressions. This is true also if there is information shared that might cause the person harm, even though it is not "negative." What we are speaking about here, however, includes any conversation about other people, even when it isn't negative. There is an old Yiddish term for someone whose conversation focuses on other people. That person is called a *yenta*. They busy themselves, curious about what is doing with this one and that one, who is going and who is coming, and the specific details of people's lives. A great person is concerned about other people for only one of two reasons: to help them or to learn from them. Any other information about other people doesn't interest them in the slightest.

In this category of speakers, we find another manner of speech, namely, complaining. In Yiddish, a *kvetch* is a groan, but a person who is "affectionately" referred to as a *kvetcher* is someone who is constantly complaining. Great people know that the more they speak positively about their situation, the more goodness that will manifest in their lives. The more a person complains, the more they are putting out negative vibrations, and that, too, will become their reality.

Ironically, Jacob is the only Torah personality who actually lost years of his life as a consequence for complaining. Our Sages point out that Jacob's life is significantly shorter than that of his father by thirty-three years. They brilliantly point out that thirty-three equals the number of words in a conversation that occurred in Jacob's later years when he stood before Pharaoh for the first time. When asked about his age, Jacob responds by saying his age and then goes on to describe his life as being one that was full of pain and suffering. For Jacob, whose whole essence was his power of speech, this was considered a shortfall in his character.

This message is especially relevant when we are having a rough day or going through a difficult time. We feel that we aren't really able to show up as our best self, and therefore have to explain and justify ourselves so that others will validate our feelings. So, we respond to an innocent "How are you?" with a full unloading of everything that is going wrong. This habit can be detrimental to our relationships and actually cause more inner turmoil, not to mention lead to gossip. We are certainly not obligated to walk around and pretend everything is amazing when we are hurting, but the more we can remain positive and optimistic in our conversations, the more that we will attract both positivity and positive people into our life.

Our mission in this world is to become lifelong learners and master conversationalists. The road to self-mastery involves us elevating our wind element and power of communication so that each conversation that we have will be filled with wisdom, clarity, truth, and positivity. We will be the ones that people will seek out when they are looking for a positive boost or to seek council and gain personal clarity. Our thought process will have its "feet on the ground" in that it will be practical and consistent but will "reach the heavens" in its breadth and vastness. Our voices will provide a breath of fresh air and be a source of life and vitality.

summary

We have seen how our thinking and communicating are the key to self-mastery over the wind element and the negative traits of idle chatter. Included in this is

- pursuing wisdom and developing the mindset of a lifelong learner,
- giving ourselves the time and space to internally process the vast amount of information that we consume and the ideas that enter into our mind,
- engaging in *pilpul*-style conversations where we further develop our ideas together with others who will challenge us and help us refine our ideas,
- refining our conversations so that they are filled with meaning rather than small talk or conversations about others.

14

FIRE (PART 1)— FEARLESS AND HUMBLE

NEFESH LEVEL/ ELEMENT	OBSTACLES	HOW TO ELEVATE	PERSONIFIED BY
Will level/Fire	Inflated ego Pursuit of power Anger	Humble and fearless leadership	Joseph Judah King David

The House of Jacob shall be fire,
and the House of Joseph flame.

Ovadiah 1:18

THE DUALITY OF GREAT LEADERS

Fear. It is what holds us back the most from being the best version of ourselves. Whether it is fear of failure, or of what others may think of you, or of losing something or someone, or just fearing the unknown, most of what stops us from taking the next major step toward our personal success is fear.

Fear stops us from taking the risks necessary to move out of the place that we are currently stuck in. Fear stops us from making the move that might advance our career and our relationships. Fear makes us feel inadequate and stops us from fully expressing ourselves. Fear causes us to stand in the back and watch life go by, instead of taking our place behind the wheel and living our life the way we truly know it should be.

In order to fully actualize our potential in this life-time, to achieve success at any level, we will need to develop the self-esteem and the self-confidence to overcome our fears and pursue our goals and dreams with passion and ambition. Our self-esteem and our confidence are rooted in the spiritual element of fire, the element of our will and motivation. Leadership, courage, and bravery are all connected to the element of fire, just as fire is always looking to rise to the top and has the ability to destroy obstacles in its way. It is therefore fearless by nature.

FEAR STOPS US FROM TAKING THE RISKS NECESSARY TO MOVE OUT OF THE PLACE THAT WE ARE CURRENTLY STUCK IN.

But the element of fire is also the root of pride and arrogance. As one becomes successful in life and overcomes obstacles, it is natural to start experiencing the swelling of the ego, which can lead one to believe that they are better than everyone else. We must therefore learn how to use the element of fire to fearlessly rise to the top but to remain modest and humble in the process.

Jim Collins, in his famous book *Good to Great*, describes a great leader as being "a study in duality: modest and willful, humble and fearless." He refers to these traits as a "duality" because while modesty and humility emphasize the smallness of the self, will and fearlessness awaken the greatness that lies within. Great leaders have the ability to excel in both of these areas.

What is their secret?

The answer is communicated to us in the final saga in the Book of Genesis: the struggle for leadership and for royalty between Jacob's children.

At the core of their strife is a budding rivalry between two of the brothers: Rachel's son Joseph and Leah's son Judah. The struggle cannot be properly understood without realizing that we are watching the emergence of two spiritual giants who will both be kings in their own right and from whom all future kings of the Jewish People will descend. Joseph and Judah will both eventually display leadership traits that will echo for all of history, but it is a messy road until they get to that place.

The story begins with Jacob showing a unique love toward Joseph. The special treatment given to Joseph, including the famous gift of a beautiful colorful cloak, is understood as Jacob's way of grooming his son Joseph to be the leader of the Jewish People. Joseph, in turn, begins to carry himself with superiority over his brothers, both in their presence as well as by reporting their flaws to Jacob. This is not received well by the brothers, who remark: "Would you then rule over us? Would you then dominate us?"[6]

Part of the reason for the brothers' hostility is that, in their minds, the true leader of the family would be Judah, and Joseph was trying to usurp a throne that was not justly his. The situation spirals out of control, and Joseph's brothers eventually send him away into slavery, a decision that seemed justified to them at the time but one they would later come to regret. He ends up in Egypt, and because of his spiritual integrity and incredible leadership abilities, he works his way up to become the viceroy of Egypt.

The trials and tribulations of both Joseph and Judah are chronicled in the Torah as we get to see the brilliance of each one of them emerge through a series of highs and lows. As Joseph is rising to power, we witness first-hand his ability to attract a following and to win over people wherever he goes. His popularity spread so much that even the great Pharaoh is asking him for advice. But instead of allowing all of his popularity to go to his head, his response is one of true level-headedness, humility, and faith: "It is not I, but God, that will see to Pharaoh's welfare."[7] This would be the attitude that Joseph would maintain throughout his reign.[8]

---

6   Genesis 37:8.

7   Ibid. 41:16.

8   See ibid. 50:19, where Yosef makes a similar statement to his brothers: "Do not fear; for am I instead of God?"

Both Joseph and Judah embody what it means to be humble and fearless leaders. In this chapter, we will focus on Joseph and discuss how to master these two traits: humility and fearlessness. We will see how they are actually both rooted in one source. In the next chapter, we will turn our attention to Judah and explore how to practically apply those traits to leading others.

THE THREE MINDSETS TO DEVELOP SELF-ESTEEM

In many ways, the story of Joseph is the ultimate rags-to-riches story. He has power, wealth, and good looks, and all because of his own sweat and tears. He's been rejected and thrown down and has overcome it all. But rather than taking the credit, he realizes that this was all the Hand of God. He can overcome every single challenge because God is with him. There is nothing to be afraid of. And he remains absolutely humble because he knows that God can take it all away.

While humility and fearlessness might seem to be a duality, in truth they go hand-in-hand. Humility does not mean that one doesn't think highly of themselves or realize their own self-worth. On the contrary, it is because of their deep appreciation of their own self-worth that they do not need to create any external façade or showcase their accomplishments to feel worthy. Being humble is about recognizing that we—and every other human being that we encounter—has a greatness within us that comes from the spark of God that is inside of us; that we have been given special gifts that, rather than taking excessive pride in, we should take great pleasure in and feel overwhelming gratitude for.

> BEING HUMBLE IS ABOUT RECOGNIZING THAT WE HAVE BEEN GIVEN SPECIAL GIFTS THAT WE SHOULD TAKE GREAT PLEASURE IN AND FEEL OVERWHELMING GRATITUDE FOR.

To become humble and fearless, it is, therefore, necessary to develop a healthy self-esteem by internalizing the following three mindsets:

1. Self-worth: I am worth something because I am a spark of God. I am worthy and have every right to live an amazing life.
2. Self-acceptance: I completely accept myself for who I am. I understand that my strengths and weaknesses are not of my own

doing but are a gift from God for me to work with, work on, and develop.

3. Self-confidence: I have the ability to succeed in life and become great because I am created in the image of God. I can overcome any obstacles that come my way and have nothing to be afraid of.

When we internalize these three mindsets, we develop self-esteem and an inner fire that cannot be broken by fear. When fear is holding us back from taking action, we remind ourselves that we have a force inside of us that is even stronger than the fear that is stopping us. We can take risks and we can step out of our comfort zone because we know that we are supported by something that is even bigger than ourselves. It is because we are humble enough to realize that our entire life is in God's hands; that also gives us the courage to realize that even if we fail, He will be there to catch us.

AWE OF GOD—THE FINAL STEP

With the understanding that the secret to the humble and fearless leader is his realization of the Godliness that he carries inside, we now return to our Sages' seventh and final criteria in their list of achievements that we must account for when we stand at the gates of heaven: "And, beyond all these, if awe of God is his treasure, yes (i.e., he is worthy), and if not, then he is not."

This feeling of being in awe of God echoes the exact words that Joseph speaks when he is at the height of his power in Egypt, when we hear him say a very powerful statement for someone in his position of power in a corrupt country: "I have awe of God."[9]

This prompts our Sages to comment: "Most people have awe of God when they are poor, but when they are rich, they become confident in their wealth. But Joseph had awe of God when we was a slave...and only grew in his awe after he became a ruler."[10]

Awe of God keeps us humble because it reminds us that we alone are powerless and that without God we are nothing, so there really is

---

9   Ibid. 42:18.
10   *Midrash Tanchuma, Parashas Naso* 28.

nothing to be arrogant about. And it makes us fearless because we know that with God's help, we are unstoppable.

Let's take a deeper look at what awe of God means, what it feels like, and how to acquire it so that we can fully understand this powerful trait.

Awe is a difficult feeling to describe in any context. And, certainly, of the many ways we relate to God (faith, love, etc.), awe seems to be the hardest one to grasp. It is especially misunderstood because the Hebrew term for awe of God, *yiras Hashem,* is often translated as "fear of God," bringing up images of a vengeful God who punishes us if we don't listen, so we had better be afraid. But this is not the true interpretation of the term. The word "awe" is the more accurate translation of what we are meant to feel toward God, and it is something that is not frightening but absolutely beautiful, exciting, and empowering.

A wonderful description of the feeling of awe comes from by positive psychologist Barbara Fredrickson:

> *Awe happens when you come across goodness on a grand scale. You literally feel overwhelmed by greatness. By comparison, you feel small and humble. Awe makes you stop in your tracks. You are momentarily transfixed. Boundaries melt away, and you feel part of something larger than yourself.*[11]

This definition of awe beautifully captures how we should relate to God: feeling "small and humble" but also a feeling of being "part of something larger than yourself." In other words, small by comparison but great at the same time when considering that you are actually part and parcel of the greatness that you are experiencing.

Similar to fear, its distant cousin, awe, is the feeling that happens when you encounter a force that is so much larger than you that it makes you hyper-aware of your smallness in relation to it. Both fear and awe are acknowledgements that the object of your fear/awe is exerting some level of control over you, locking in your focus so intensely that everything else outside of this one source melts away.

---

11   Barbara L. Fredrickson, PhD. *Positivity* (New York: Crown Publishers, 2009).

But while fear has a negative and disempowering type of control over you—either because it forces you to do something you don't want to, or it paralyzes you from doing what you want to do—awe, on the other hand, controls you in the opposite way. Awe brings out a deep desire to come closer to this awe-inspiring force, a yearning to be greater so that we will be worthy to stand in its presence. It is a feeling that touches you deeply, creating an awakening from inside of you, an expansion of your consciousness. That is the power of awe!

AWE BRINGS OUT A DEEP DESIRE TO COME CLOSER TO THIS AWE-INSPIRING FORCE, A YEARNING TO BE GREATER SO THAT WE WILL BE WORTHY TO STAND IN ITS PRESENCE.

Think about the feeling you get when you are standing in the presence of a very great person who has accomplished something beyond your own comprehension. Think about the feeling that you get when you are witness to a magnificent scenery or something that seems breathtaking or miraculous. Think about how small we are in the big picture of creation, how we are just a speck in the universe that extends beyond our imagination both physically and spiritually, through the past, present, and future.

All of these feelings make us overwhelmed by our smallness. And that is without even thinking about God and the fact that the greatness of God is way beyond what we as humans can possibly comprehend!

But then we remind ourselves that we have a piece of God inside of us. That very same Master of the world who created the vast scenery, the miraculous moment, and the superhuman gifts is the very same God who gives life and strength to all of us! This means that as small as we are in comparison to everything we just said, we have the ability to make waves and make a difference. We are that butterfly that flaps its wings and creates massive movement across the world. Just as when we are standing before a great landscape in awe of how beautiful the world can be, we become in awe of the person that we can be. And that pushes us forward in the most powerful way. This is the richest, most exciting, and most empowering feeling that we can have. Experiencing the vastness of our own potential, our Godly potential, is the greatest experience of awe possible!

There are certainly those who might find this difficult. Perhaps when they contemplate God, they are not filled with awe and are therefore equally uninspired by the idea that there is Godliness inside of them. Or perhaps their self-esteem is so low that they are unable to truly believe that there is Godliness inside of them. A practical tool for them is to follow the advice given by the great Sage, Rabbi Akiva. On the Torah verse that instructs us "of your God, you shall have awe," Rabbi Akiva comments that "this verse comes to include people of great wisdom."[12] This means that often, to develop a sense of awe, we can envision people whom we are aware of who awaken inside of us feelings of awe. Most people can name at least a handful of people in their life who have made a deep impact on them or who have inspired them in some way.

We could be complacent to say, "That is them, but I can't be like that." Or, as we said above, we can view ourselves "as part of that greatness" with the belief that the same fire that burns inside of them can be transferred to us. Of the four elements, it is the element of fire that spreads the easiest. A small wick coming into contact with a fire will immediately catch some of its flame.

A great exercise, then, is to have a list of five to ten of the most inspiring people that you have encountered in your life. This can include both people that you have met in person, people that you have read about, encountered their work, or any other way that you have come across them. Next to each of their names, write two or three things that you admire about them, things that you would love to see as part of yourself.

Whenever you are facing fear or lacking motivation, use this list to envision greatness and bring yourself to a place of awe. Imagine that some of their fire is rubbing off on you, and remind yourself that you, too, can be great like them.

WHAT IS YOUR TREASURE?

We saw above that the corruption of the element of fire and the struggle of arrogance and ego is connected to Sodom, a city of much

---

12   Talmud, *Pesachim* 22b.

beauty and wealth, which caused them to think of themselves as better than everyone else and therefore inhospitable to anyone who came their way. Their affluence caused them to forget about God, rather than realizing where the blessing came from.

This is what our Sages refer to when they say: "Most people have awe of God when they are poor, but when they are rich, they become confident in their wealth. But Joseph had awe of God when he was a slave…and only grew in his awe after he became a ruler."

Our Sages' observation that awe of God becomes harder and harder as one climbs the ladder of wealth and power still holds true today. There are those who become successful, and as they grow in their wealth, their egos also swell. Yet, there are those whose souls and character seem to grow along with their wealth. Wealth can either change a person and hurt their character or place a person in a position where they can make a massive impact on others. Whereas a big ego serves as a barrier to one connecting spiritually and moves them farther away from accomplishing their mission, a big sense of self-worth and responsibility will lead a person to making a tremendous positive impact on the world.

Perhaps this is why our Sages specifically use the following language when speaking of the afterlife: "If awe of God **is his treasure,** he is worthy," evoking the imagery that rather than taking pride in his early treasure of wealth or power, his true treasure is his genuine accomplishments.

This line seems to echo another idea that we find elsewhere in the Talmud, "The Holy One, blessed be He, has nothing in His treasury other than a treasure of awe of Heaven."[13] Again, we see "awe of God" associated with a treasure house and what seems to be the only item contained in God's very own treasure house. The repeated association of "awe of God" with a treasure seems to be our Sages way of reminding us that unlike this physical world, which recognizes shiny items, large homes, and luxurious experiences as symbols of wealth, in the Next World, the only thing that will matter is one's genuine accomplishments.

---

13   Talmud, *Berachos* 33b.

The following story illustrates that there is only one treasure that we can take with us into the Next World:

While lying on his deathbed, a wealthy and very-well respected man handed his children two sealed envelopes. He instructed them to open one as soon as he died and the other as soon as he was buried. He died a short while later and, in respecting his wishes, his children opened the first envelope. In it, they found the following message:

"My dear children, I know that you will do your very best to ensure that I have a funeral that is becoming for someone who lived a life like the one that I had. I do have one request about my burial, though." The children all leaned in a bit closer to hear what it is that this honorable man, who accomplished so much in his lifetime, is requesting. "Please bury me wearing my favorite pair of socks."

The children look at one another with puzzled looks on their faces. Despite the confusion they felt from such an unusual request, they would attempt to honor it. They informed the burial society about the request, but, in conforming with Jewish tradition that the deceased is buried only with shrouds, they were unsuccessful in convincing them to allow the once-powerful man to be buried in his socks.

After the funeral and the laying of their beloved and sockless dad to rest, the children opened up the second letter. In it, he wrote, "I am well-aware that you were unable to bury me wearing my socks, since it goes against Jewish tradition. It is my sincere wish for you that you have learned a powerful lesson from this ordeal. I have spent my entire life amassing a great fortune, power, and many possessions. I had no problem getting anyone and everyone to do whatever I pleased. Yet, it has all come down to this. I cannot even take my favorite pair of socks with me to the Next World! Please never forget the things that really matter."

This is what it means when it says, "The Holy One, blessed be He, has nothing in His treasury other than fear of Heaven." The only absolute acquisition in this world that actually comes with us to the next one is whether we discovered what it means to live genuinely in this world, the feeling that occurs when you are in tune with your inner spark. It is this amazing and beautiful feeling that is magnified in the Next World when there is nothing separating us from fully experiencing the highest levels of our soul.

summary

We have seen how humility and fearlessness are the key to self-mastery over the fire element and the negative traits of arrogance. Included in this is

- developing a healthy self-esteem by practicing the three mind-sets of self-worth, self-acceptance, and self-confidence;
- developing the trait of awe of God by contemplating the greatness of God, and how we are both small in His presence but also contain a spark of Godliness inside of us;
- making a list of the people that inspire us most, as well as in what ways we wish to emulate them and envisioning catching some of their fire.

15
FIRE (PART 2)—
TRAITS OF GREAT LEADERS

NEFESH LEVEL/ ELEMENT	OBSTACLES	HOW TO ELEVATE	PERSONIFIED BY
Will level/Fire	Inflated ego Pursuit of power Anger	Humble and fearless leadership	Joseph Judah King David

The effect of humility is awe of God,
wealth, honor, and life.

Proverbs 22:4

THE LEADER IN YOU

Each and every one of us has the potential to be a great leader. And the world needs great leaders.

Some people find themselves in a very clear leadership capacity in their careers or communities. Spouses and parents have a leadership role with the people in their household. Beyond this, every one of us will be presented with unique circumstances as part of our life mission that will provide us the opportunity to flex our leadership muscles.

In the last chapter, we focused on the two main qualities of being a great leader: being humble and being fearless. Humility is the correction of the trait of arrogance that is rooted in the element of fire, and fearlessness is the element of fire being used properly. In this chapter, we will focus on applying those practically and showing how great leaders inspire, empower, and communicate with those that they are leading.

For this, we turn our attention to the Torah's other archetype of a great leader: Judah.

Judah was viewed by the brothers as their leader. It was he who had the final say in the sale of Joseph. And while Joseph is going through his turmoil and ascending from rags to riches, his brother Judah is going through his own struggles. The persistent pain and mourning of Jacob after losing his beloved son Joseph is a constant reminder to the brothers of the whole ordeal, ultimately causing them to question Judah's leadership.[1] This, as well as personal ordeals that Judah is going through in his own family, teach Judah the important lesson that even great leaders will make mistakes.

The two brothers finally unite when the brothers descend to Egypt to purchase food in a time of famine. They find themselves face-to-face with their long-lost brother, now the viceroy of the only land with any food left, thanks to Joseph's vision and wisdom. Joseph doesn't immediately reveal his identity but instead shows the brothers hostility in a ruse to try to see whether they have changed. Part of doing so is threatening to incarcerate the youngest of Jacob's sons, Benjamin. Joseph is waiting to see if they will turn their back on Benjamin the way they did to him so many years before.

Judah takes a strong leadership role, giving the viceroy an ultimatum to either take him as captive in Benjamin's place or get ready for an all-out brawl. Acting as the spokesperson for the brothers,

---

1   *Rashi*, Genesis 38:1.

Judah also admits that the brothers misjudged Joseph and treated him unfairly. This leads to that powerful moment when Joseph reveals himself and the brothers reunite.

In Judah, we find a very real portrait of what it means to be a great leader. We see that the road to greatness involves early failures and questionable decisions. It requires realizing where you made mistakes, picking yourself up, dusting yourself off, and moving on. It requires taking responsibility for what happened in the past and what will happen in the future.

In fact, the very name Judah captures the essence of the personality of the fearless and humble leader. It is also where the Jewish People get their name from. The name Judah in Hebrew is *Yehudah*. The word "Jew" comes from the Hebrew word *Yehudi* (a Judaean).

The root of the name Yehudah is the word *hod*, which is literally translated as splendor, a word very appropriate for royalty. But when we take a look at some of the other words that contain *hod* at their root, a more targeted understanding of the word begins to develop. *Hod* is found at the root of the following words:

1. *Hodu*—used in prayer as an expression of giving praise
2. *Modeh* or *todah*—giving gratitude
3. *Modeh*—also means to admit when you have done something wrong
4. *Hod*—The word *hod* itself is translated in certain contexts as empathy; the ability to deeply listen to someone and/or to feel their pain

All of these words share something in common. They are all traits that require a person to make themselves small in the presence of another.

The name Yehudah was given to him precisely because his mother Leah was thanking God for the gift of a fourth child: "This time, let me praise (*odeh*) God."[2] And what an appropriate name for the one who would become known as one who can openly admit when they are wrong.

---

2   Genesis 29:35.

HABITS OF HUMBLE LEADERS

PRAISE AND THANKS

Praising and thanking are both ways of building someone up and acknowledging that you look up to them and need them. Great leaders, parents, bosses, and managers make it a habit to look for reasons to praise and compliment others. Those around them are therefore always trying to perform better because they know that they will be recognized.

GREAT LEADERS, PARENTS, BOSSES, AND MANAGERS MAKE IT A HABIT TO LOOK FOR REASONS TO PRAISE AND COMPLIMENT OTHERS.

This is a great principle to live with. The more a leader compliments, the more the people around him will do things in order to be recognized. A spouse or parent who freely compliments and shows gratitude will see how the people in their home will surprise them and do more and more to reap the great pleasure of the appreciation and praise that they can rely on. Everybody enjoys a compliment, no matter who they are.

My wife has a habit, which I try to emulate, that has been a game-changer for our family: each night when she wishes our children a good night, she adds on a "thank you" or a compliment for something that that child did that day. Because it is a habit, it comes totally natural to her. Imagine the feeling that the children have when they go to sleep with the last thing that they have heard being something positive about themselves.

Criticism, on the other hand, does not come from humility but from arrogance and therefore never, ever helps. Many relationships have been ruined by spouses or parents who have made it a habit to communicate their needs through subtle criticisms and slights that disempower the other person and undermine the relationship. Though these micro-insults seem small at the time, they snowball until the relationship begins to come apart. In the short-term, the one who is demanding might get the results they wanted, but it comes at the price of the relationship. Imagine poking one tiny hole in the side of a boat. And then another. And then another. It won't take long until that boat begins to sink. That is what happens every time we drop even the slightest criticism. It is another small hole in the boat.

The great, humble leader understands how to point out the shortcomings in the performance of others without it coming across as putting them down. Instead, he or she will figure out how to empower them to the point that they will come to realize that their performance wasn't up to the standard that is **needed of them** and for which they are being relied upon. Let's take a look at two examples:

- An important task was neglected, e.g., the employee didn't send the email, the child did not do the chore, the spouse didn't take care of the errand, etc. The great humble leader will hold the other accountable—not by making them feel irresponsible but by letting them know how much they are relied upon and needed. When pointing out the shortcoming in their performance, the language of "you didn't do what you were supposed to do" is replaced with "just reminding you how much I need you and rely on you to..." In fact, the more that you can emphasize your need rather than something they did wrong, the better.

- The employee/child/spouse is showing behaviors that are below acceptable standard. The great humble leader doesn't enforce the behavior by pointing out its recurring nature with words like "you always..." or "you never..." or "this is just like you to..." On the contrary, the language that is used will be more along the lines of "is something wrong? It is so not like you to..." By using this language, you are simultaneously empowering the person and pointing out the shortfall. In their heads, they feel good by the fact that you are not identifying them with this lower standard, and they therefore want to live up to what they believe you think of them.

VULNERABILITY

The next word that derives its root from *hod* is to admit. Admission is certainly an act of making yourself smaller. Great humble leaders are the first to admit when they don't know or have made a mistake. They are comfortable enough with themselves to be vulnerable with others. Because of their healthy self-esteem, they don't view vulnerability as a sign of weakness.

In truth, vulnerability is a sign of courage. It creates inside of us an attitude of always learning and always growing. It allows us to enlist others in the process. This will further expand our capacity to tap into the collective wisdom of others and keep on innovating. When we allow our walls to come down, others do as well, and this creates a whole environment of growth and collective learning. People are motivated to support one another and grow together.

Great humble leaders have found that the best way to motivate is to present the circumstances or conflict before having decided on a solution, and in a way that it becomes clear to the employee/child/spouse that you truly believe that he can come up with the perfect solution on his own. Instead of being met with resentment, excuses, procrastination, and laziness, this way empowers them to volunteer their services, come up with creative solutions, and access the necessary resources. It empowers them to take responsibility. The very feeling of taking on responsibility makes people relate to a task—not as a job for someone else but as an extension of themselves.

EMPATHETIC LISTENING

It is for this reason that humble leaders also make good listeners. They listen with an empathetic ear, allowing themselves to fully connect with and experience the person speaking to them. The opposite of humble, empathetic listening is listening that is all about giving advice or solving the other person's problem. Before they even have a chance to finish, the more arrogant listener will cut them off to share his brilliance, never fully processing the subtleties and the feelings behind what is being expressed. The humble listener is sensitive to all of this and becomes fully connected with the emotions of the speaker, whether or not they on their own would have those emotions.

There is a very humorous but truthful video that went viral that illustrates the need that some people have to just be heard. A woman is sitting on a couch complaining to her husband about the terrible headaches that she is having. The camera zooms in, and we see that there is actually (and quite comically) a big metal nail wedged smack in the middle of the wife's forehead!

The husband innocently suggests that perhaps if she took the nail out of her forehead, her headache would cease. The wife practically ignores his comment and proceeds to complain about her head hurting. The husband repeats his suggestion again, this time slower and louder, assuming that this time his very obvious advice might be received. But instead, the wife gets frustrated that her husband is not doing a good enough job listening to her and is just trying to force his opinion on her. The husband now gets frustrated and insists that he is listening, and is very sure that if she would just listen to him, her issue would be resolved. The video ends with the issue unresolved but a couple quite frustrated with one another.

Many couples who watch this video find that it deeply resonates with them. Putting aside the obvious satirical nature of the specific problem that this couple is dealing with, the mode of communication that is happening between the two is something that many couples deal with. This emphasizes the importance of learning how to listen and withholding comments and judgments, even when we think we know.

SLOW-TEMPERED

A core habit of the great humble leader is the ability to restrain themselves from losing their temper. Losing one's temper is connected to the destructive nature of the element of fire and is indeed the most destructive force that is contained in all of the attributes of our personality.

Judah was appointed to royalty even though he was not the oldest in the family. His older brothers were passed over precisely because of their tempers.[3] The great humble leader knows how to develop the mindsets and the habits that are necessary to disengage and pivot from a situation where they feel that their temper is brewing.

We lose our tempers because we feel disrespected and that our ego is being slighted. In other words, our fire element is under attack. It

---

3   See Genesis 49:8 and the commentary of *Rashi*.

is precisely because the element of fire inside is under attack that it reinforces itself in the form of anger. This is why those without healthy self-esteem are more likely to lose their temper. The great humble leader understands how to reinforce their element of fire in a positive way by reinforcing the mindsets that we spoke about earlier: self-worth, self-acceptance, and self-confidence. They remind themselves of their inherent worth and abilities and reaccept themselves, despite how the other person is making them feel.

TAKING RESPONSIBILITY

Using the element of fire properly means showing courage and never shying away from taking responsibility at a time when one should, rationalizing that it is because of humility. At the moment that Judah was ready to put himself on the line for his brother Benjamin, that was the moment when he truly earned his place as the leader of the brothers. Our Sages teach us: "Where there are no men, strive to be the man."[4]

We are all presented with opportunities in our life to be leaders by taking responsibility. It is part of our mission. If we capitalize, then we will feel the tremendous satisfaction of actualizing our potential and making our impact. If not, then we will live a life of trying to compensate with false pride and an ego that is so fragile that it can bring us crashing down with even the slightest insult. The fearless and humble leader, on the other hand, is powerful and unbreakable because his strength comes from an authentic place—inside himself.

KING DAVID

Our discussion about Judah and leadership would certainly be incomplete without giving our attention to another humble and fearless leader who completed the story of Judah. It is from the royal dynasty of Judah that the great King David, and the entire Davidic dynasty, descended from many generations later. King David is the quintessential humble and fearless leader. The stories of David feature many times

---

4   *Avos* 2:5.

where David errs and, immediately upon recognizing his mistake, he admits and repents. Many sections in his book of Psalms are dedicated to themes of humility and repentance,[5] and King David is well known for the bravery he showed that gained him great renown in the incident of slaying the mighty warrior, Goliath.

In addition to being a descendant of Judah, David's roots are found elsewhere in the Torah as well. We saw above how the city of Sodom is the Torah's archetype of the corruption of the element of fire and was therefore destroyed with fire. The only survivors of that experience were Abraham's nephew Lot and his daughters. It from their lineage that a great woman would be born: the righteous Moabite princess, Ruth, who would go on to be the grandmother of King David. David, therefore, embodies the elevation of the fire element; his very roots being connected to both the city of Sodom as well as the tribe of Judah!

Our Sages point this out in their comments on a verse in Psalms that states: "I [God] 'found' David, my servant," prompting our Sages to comment: "Where did [God] find him? In Sodom!"[6] With these words, our Sages are alluding to the fact that the very potential of the people of Sodom that they corrupted would become the DNA for a true leader, David.

We see from here that it is through Judah and his descendants that the true elevation of the element of fire comes, turning the affluence and the arrogance of Sodom into the humility and fearlessness that are necessary to accomplish one's mission.

summary

We have seen how developing the habits of humble and fearless leadership are the keys to self-mastery over the fire element. Included in these habits are:

- praising, thanking, and empowering others, rather than criticizing;

---

5   See Psalms 10, 22, and 51, just to name a few.
6   *Bereishis Rabbah* 50:10.

- being vulnerable and having the ability to admit when you are wrong or do not know;
- learning how to be an empathetic listener;
- learning to control one's temper;
- stepping up and taking responsibility when necessary.

16

FOUR ELEMENTS AND PERSONALITY TYPES

Just as no two faces are completely identical
to each other, so too, no two personalities
are identical to each other.

Midrash Tanchuma, Pinchas 10

THE FOUR ELEMENTS AND YOU

Congratulations on reaching this point in our journey! We have now explored the qualities that are necessary to reach mastery over the four inner elements of our *nefesh*, which is the central focus of our mission in this world. We have seen the importance of living with energy, joy, routine, and an abundance mindset. We have demonstrated how pleasure is meant to be channeled toward building deep, loving relationships that will be eternal. We have explored the importance of always searching for truth and becoming a lifelong learner, and we have shown that we all have the ability to become humble and fearless leaders.

We have met the Torah personalities that represent these qualities. And we have examined how through elevating the four inner elements, we are also achieving the accomplishments that will be asked of us when we move on to the Next World.

Let's review these connections once more:

NEFESH LEVEL	HOW TO ELEVATE	PERSONIFIED BY	END OF LIFE QUESTION
Body level (earth)	Energy Joy Consistency of habit Abundance mindset	Abraham and Sarah (Rebecca)	"Did you do your work with faith?" "Did you establish habits of Torah?"
Feeling level (water)	Channeled pleasure Deep love Hope	Isaac and Rebecca	"Did you engage in 'being fruitful and multiplying?'" "Did you hope for deliverance?"
Intellectual level (wind)	Intellectual honesty Pursuit of truth Lifelong learning Meaningful communication	Jacob Rachel and Leah	"Did you engage in the discussions of wisdom?" "Did you understand one matter from another?"
Will level (fire)	Humble and fearless Leadership	Joseph Judah King David	Awe of God is your treasure

All human beings have these four inner elements, and we all struggle with the four human struggles that are connected to each level. In that sense, we are all the same. However, no two people experience the strengths or the struggles the same way. Each one of our journeys is dramatically different.

This is one of the fascinating aspects of being human. Just like our faces are all different, despite the fact that we all have the same combination of facial features, it is the very small subtleties that create a human race where each individual is dramatically different from the other. What is true about the outer world is true about the inner world as well.

In this chapter, we will turn our attention to explore how the four elements differ in every single person, and how, once we have explored each element—and the struggles and qualities that are connected to each of them—it is our task to look inward and ask ourselves how they operate inside each of us individually.

EXTROVERTS, INTROVERTS, AND EVERYTHING IN BETWEEN

As we discovered our inner worlds through the lens of the stories in the Book of Genesis, we also met different Torah personalities and how their personal attributes and life stories made them the most suited to be engaged in their specific struggles. The Torah does not present us with faceless heroes doing great things. On the contrary, the Torah focuses on the specific successes and struggles that related to their individual character to really paint a picture for us of who this personality was.

An example of this might be the contrast between Abraham and Isaac. There we find a very stark contrast between two great personalities. Our Sages teach us that despite the fact that they were father and son and looked almost identical, their dominant traits were very different from one another. As we saw, the trait of Abraham focused on his enthusiasm, joy, and generosity to all, while Isaac embodies the trait of inner discipline and a much more targeted love.

It is impossible to say what it would have been like to meet Abraham or Isaac in person. But one does get the sense that the Torah is trying to portray Abraham as a dynamic, outgoing personality whose home is open to all and who sits in the front of his tent making conversation with passersby. He is a charismatic teacher with many students and a strong leader with many followers, a lover of all and beloved by all who meet him.

And then we meet Isaac, and a very different picture emerges. We envision a man of spiritual intensity that is so strong he is ready to give up his life for it. We hear him speak much less than we heard from his father, but are tuned in much more to his emotions, especially the deep love for his wife. One might conjecture—though we can never really be sure—that Isaac is by nature a more inward-focused individual, living in the inner world of feelings, self-reflection, and introspection.

One could easily see how, when reading the Torah, someone with a much more outgoing social personality would find connection with the stories of Abraham. It is easy to get excited and inspired by a personality like Abraham, as so many people dream of being the dynamic, charismatic, and outgoing leader who can capture the attention of others with their dynamism.

A more inward-focused person might feel a stronger connection with Isaac's way of life. Seeing how Isaac's more inward nature is because of his deep sensitivity might resonate with many people who do not have large personalities and are often labeled (or mislabeled) as shy, introverted, or antisocial. Often, a quieter person might live with a fear that they won't be noticed and that their voice will not be heard.

Through the lens of Isaac, they will come to understand that quieter types are often actually much more in tune with their emotions and inner-strength. They might be more sensitive and have a better understanding of their own feelings and that of others, so that you might find yourself more inclined to have a deep heart-to-heart with them. Often, they are less distracted by the buzz of social activity around them and therefore accomplish more with the time that they have. They are intentional, calculated, and productive.

And then there will be those who are not necessarily charismatic change-the-world types *or* the disciplined inwardly focused type, but find a strong connection to the truth-seeking, always-growing, always-adapting-to-what-life-throws-at-them person that can be found in Jacob. As we learn more and more about the various personalities in the Torah, we might find ourselves more drawn to certain Torah personalities or stories than others precisely because the Torah is supposed to speak to every individual, whoever they are and wherever their life takes them. This does not negate the fact that we are supposed to learn from every story and every Torah personality, but some hit deeper than others.

This same principle holds true with the four inner elements. As we explore the four inner elements and reflect on our own life, we might find that even though we all have the four elements inside of us, we might have more of the strengths or struggles of one of the elements than the others. This realization is crucial to our growth. When we understand how the inner elements work, we gain the self-awareness to quickly and accurately pinpoint why we behave in a certain way and what we need to work on. It will help us in our self-growth, our relationships, and in choosing a path in life that truly fits us. And the moment that we become aware of any strong inner pull in one specific area, that is the greatest indication that we have begun to uncover our mission!

THE FOUR ELEMENTS PERSONALITY SYSTEM

In the last century, the concept of personality types became a main-stream focus in the world of psychology. Understanding people as either "introverts" or "extroverts," "Type A" or "Type B," and "right-brained" or "left-brained" has become a common way to try to understand our-selves and our personalities. There are many personality systems and assessments that have opened our eyes to patterns in our behavior that can help us tap into our strengths and identify our weaknesses. While there is always a danger of putting oneself "in a box" or blindly applying a premade profile to ourselves, with a proper understanding and analy-sis, it can help us gain greater insight into ourselves and point out what to look for. A personality system will often tell us things that we already know about ourselves, but seeing it categorized and articulated will give us a better grasp of it and how to apply our strengths and weaknesses.

The personality system that is most rooted in Jewish principles is one that is rooted in the four elements of our inner world. To reiterate, we all have all four realms inside of us, yet different people will find that some of those forces are more powerful inside them than the others. We therefore don't want to label anyone as being "rooted" in one ele-ment. Instead, we want to figure out in what area we are the strongest, then second, then third, then fourth. That means that there are really several possible combinations, and it would require a whole book unto itself to explore each one. But let's take a brief look at what aspects of one's personality might indicate which of the four elements is most dominant in a person:

THE DOMINANT EARTH ELEMENT

A person who has strong earth/body level tendencies is one who is very "down-to-earth," practical, and a realist. This is because the earth element is the realm that is most concerned with survival and the basics that we need for living. That concern used positively creates an individual who is well-grounded and firmly planted, resulting in them being well-organized, dependable, and consistent. They are most comfortable "playing by the rules" in any given situation and prefer a structured environment. Someone with these tendencies will thrive in an organizational role or taking an idea and executing it to perfection. It can also lead to being stubborn, or very meticulous, or set in one's ways. As we said earlier, someone with an excess of the earth element might feel insecure at times, which can lead to depression and jealousy of others. If that is the case, this person must use their earth element to counteract that in the ways we discussed earlier—by doing the outer movements that will ignite feelings of joy and love.

THE DOMINANT WATER ELEMENT

A person with strong water/feeling level tendencies is typically described as being very emotionally driven. They are very much in touch with others' feelings and will show much affection. They are also deeply affected by their emotions so that they will react with stronger emotions than others. They thrive from their relationships: the outgoing ones from being around lots of people, and the more introverted ones from their personal conversations with others. Someone with strong water tendencies might be found as a teacher for young children or working with an underprivileged population. They might also be inclined to volunteer for charities. Someone with strong water tendencies who is not feeling connected emotionally might turn to physical pleasure to supplement a feeling of emptiness inside. They could be at risk of becoming addicted. It is so important for someone with strong water tendencies to have a strong support group or a deep relationship with a friend or spouse.

THE DOMINANT AIR ELEMENT

A person with strong tendencies in the intellectual/communicating level are often described as either very brilliant or very creative, but certainly as ones who live in their head. They are curious, love to learn new information, and problem-solve. Because the thinking level is also connected to communication, a person at this level is typically driven to want to share that knowledge with others, either through teaching, writing, or creating. They typically become professors, philosophers, writers, poets, or take on other creative pursuits. The dangers associated with these tendencies is that if their interests are not being channeled toward important wisdom, they can drift into exploring more frivolous and sometimes even destructive matters. Additionally, a struggle of this personality type is often lack of consistency and frequent changing of mind.

THE DOMINANT FIRE ELEMENT

And finally, those with strong fire/motivation tendencies are often described as highly motivated and big doers. They look to start new projects and build their empires. They are not bound by people telling them what they can and cannot do, so they might be the first to break rules but also to accomplish things that others have never accomplished before. Because of this, they might come across as being too full of themselves or impatient with others, especially soft personalities. Fire personalities are typically found as founders or CEOs of companies or launching new initiatives to make the world a better place. A struggle of those with fire tendencies can be big egos and/or very rough personalities. They might get frustrated with others when things are not going their way. They must learn to become leaders rather than dictators.

IF YOU FEEL THAT YOU HAVE AN OVERLOAD OF ONE SPECIFIC WEAKNESS, IT IS QUITE LIKELY THAT THIS SPECIFIC TRAIT IS SOMEHOW INTERTWINED WITH YOUR MISSION IN THE WORLD.

So, while we all have the same inner elements, how they express themselves in each of us varies significantly. Every individual is gifted in this world with some areas that they are naturally strong at and some that they struggle with. Over the course of our time in this world, we are meant to refine our traits so that the strong ones become even stronger and so that we are improving on the traits that we struggle with. Once a person has become comfortable with who they are as a person, we can begin to embark on living a life where they will successfully accomplish their mission.

If you feel that you have an overload of one specific weakness that haunts you more than the others, a trait that makes you fall again and again, and it seems that there is no shortage of triggers for this behavior, it is quite likely that this specific trait is somehow intertwined with your mission in the world. It is through working on this specific trait that you will accomplish your purpose in this world. It is precisely these struggles that will build your character, teach you life lessons, and lead you to success in the future. As we mentioned above from the great Chassidic master Rav Tzadok: "In the areas that a person struggles and repeatedly falls, it is in those areas that he is destined for greatness."[1]

It is also important that even if we identify one area of strength or weakness and realize that that is what we need to be working on, we don't end up neglecting other areas of growth. No matter what specific area you were put here to work on, it is all in the context of building yourself up as a full human being.

This concept is beautifully illustrated by this wonderful quote from an amazing work on Jewish spirituality called *Building a Sanctuary in my Heart*. The author writes:

> *One can talk about fixing something when, for example, there is a house that has something damaged, such as a wall, a door, or the like. Then, one can say that the damage must be repaired. But if there isn't even a house, there is no need to fix anything. You first need a house, and then, there can be a need to fix it. This is also the case with our purpose in this world. Even if, in fact, a person has come down here to rectify something in particular, that does not mean that [paraphrased] his entire work starts and finishes there. Rather, each person must first develop himself, building in his soul a well-founded structure.[2]*

---

1   *Tzidkas Hatzaddik* §49.
2   *Building a Sanctuary in my Heart*, chap. 4.

The author's metaphor of comparing building our inner world to building a house is extremely powerful. Like the four walls of a room, each one of the four elements come together to create a wholeness that is inside of us. Some of those will take more effort to perfect and some of them less, but when we do, we have built ourselves a beautiful and complete entity.

THE FOUR ELEMENTS IN RELATIONSHIPS

Understanding how the different elements differ inside of us plays a major role in how we relate to others. It can help us understand our loved ones, acquaintances, and people that we work with and how they are wired. Relationships between individuals who have different dominant inner elements can be either the greatest blessing or the greatest struggle, depending on how well they understand where the other person is coming from. With proper perspective, the different personalities might balance each other out and create great harmony. Without that, it can lead to misunderstanding, confusion, and frustration.

Let's see a few examples:

- A dominant fire personality and dominant earth personality might make very good partners if they understand each other. The fire is passionate and ambitious but can also be impulsive and over-ambitious. The earth personality is more grounded and practical, carefully weighing the outcomes of the various decisions. With mutual respect, they will balance one another out, with the fire personality shooting for the stars and the earth personality charting out a realistic course of action. If both personalities are extreme, disaster will strike as the dominant fire personality will get frustrated and lash out at the partner, whose earth element will cause him to shut down and lose all motivation.

- A group of friends might sit down to map out a vacation together. The dominant fire personality wants to make the most of every moment by doing all sorts of activities and bucket-list items that will be thrilling and exciting. The dominant air personality is interested in discovering new places and learning new things, complacent to do less but experience things in very qualitative manner. The dominant water personality is interested in a relaxing and pleasurable environment where they can catch up with friends or spend meaningful time with loved ones. The dominant earth personality wants to make sure that things are well-organized and properly planned out, attending to the details of the trip and assuring that accommodations and food are well-considered and taken care of.

- A husband and wife find that they are constantly disagreeing about attending events that they are invited to. One of the spouses is a dominant water personality and feels responsible to attend in order to maintain certain relationships and not disappoint others. The dominant air personality sees the events as pointless and is questioning the logic behind spending time engaging in activity just to please someone else. In another marriage, the dominant earth personality lacks the energy and enthusiasm to go out and would prefer to stay home and stick to routine. The dominant fire personality will want to go if there is opportunity to network and accomplish something.

These are just a few general examples of how different personalities with dominant traits might respond to different situations. To reiterate, it is important not to just identify the dominant trait but the secondary and tertiary traits as well, as they will also play a role in a person's individual preferences.

As we become more self-aware of how the elements operate inside of us, as well as how they operate in others, we become more aware of our relationship dynamics and more adept at managing through the complications and sticky situations that evolve. We become more tolerant and less judgmental of others and, even more importantly, not as hard on ourselves.

summary

We have seen how the four elements differ from person to person, how they express themselves, and the more one knows themselves, the more it affects their personal growth and relationships. It is therefore necessary to

- become more and more self-aware of how we operate and interact with the world (this happens naturally [when we are paying attention] as well as by learning about the different categories of human personality and applying them to ourselves);
- identify which of the four inner elements are most dominant inside of us, which are secondary and so on, and how they manifest in our life.

17

DISCOVERING YOUR SUPERPOWERS

*I was created now because the time
has come that I am needed to perfect
some aspect of the world. If I remain
focused on the purpose that I was created,
I am worthy, but if not, it is as if
I never came onto this world.*

Rabbi Avraham Yitzchak Hakohen Kook

THE BLESSING OF INDIVIDUALITY

There is a beautiful custom in Jewish homes for parents to bless their children on Friday night as Shabbat sets in. The blessing takes only a few moments, but it is a time of very close connection between parent and child, as each parent places his or her hands on the head of each child individually and blesses them with the blessing of peace. Often, parents will take a few extra moments and add to the blessing words of affection and compliments. After a long week of coming and going, of ups and downs, when so much of the communication between parents and children is based on making sure they are doing what they need to be doing and completing what needed to get done, this moment of blessing transitions the family into a new space. It is a moment where each child feels accepted and loved for who they are: unique and special individuals.

The custom is based on the final scene of the Book of Genesis. The patriarch Jacob is on his deathbed and calls his children, all of them now reunited, together to bless them. His blessings are quite unusual, though, as they seem to be more of descriptions of the unique characteristics of each one of them than actual blessings. He speaks about the leadership gifts of Judah, the poetic nature of Naftali, the scholarship of Issachar, the business-savvy of Zebulun, and the military-proclivity of the tribe of Dan. In some instances, he doesn't even mention their strengths, but only references their struggles, such as the impulsiveness of Reuben or the wrath of Simon. Through the blessings of Jacob, we learn a powerful lesson about the importance of recognizing one's individuality.

In the opening chapter, we discussed that our mission in life involves both an inner journey and an outer journey. Throughout our discussion, we have seen that the entire book of Genesis is really an instruction manual about how to accomplish our mission. Each story taught us another lesson about how to build up our inner world. Now, with the foundation strong, our attention is called to the important work of identifying the very specific unique gifts that we are given and seeing how we are meant to use them to impact the world, to make the external journey one that is dynamic and meaningful.

The final story in Genesis gives us a glimpse of twelve brothers, each called upon to fill a different role. The number twelve in the Torah is meant to signify a complete community, like the twelve edges in a three-dimensional object. The lesson is that it is only when each individual is utilizing the special gifts that they have been given can the world be considered complete. Without you being you, there will be a void in the wholeness of the world.

Jacob lived the life of an extremely devoted parent and understood the depth of each of his children. He had the ability to look deeply into the eyes and hearts of each of his children and to see what their mission in life was. He understood in which areas each of his children could take on leadership roles. He stayed connected to all of his children, no matter what they did, and saw all their different sides. And, in his final conversation with each one, he gives them the greatest blessing—the secret to what makes each one unique. A blessing is more than just a mystical incantation bestowing good luck. By being able to look deeply into another and share with them their strengths and weaknesses in the most honest, personal, and loving way, you are giving them the greatest gift, a blessing that sets them on a path to truly be themselves.

In this chapter, we will turn our attention to how to discover our individual gifts, our unique path of life, and how we are meant to impact the world.

DISCOVERING THE ROAD YOU SHOULD TAKE

Whether you are a career professional, entrepreneur, student, intern, stay-at-home parent, or professional volunteer, how you spend your days is going to be one of the main ways to make your mark on this world. Our occupation (which, for the sake of this chapter, includes both the paid and not-paid ways a person invests their days) is where we invest the bulk of our time, and it is hopefully the place where we invest our brain power, innovation, creativity, and ambition. It is the avenue through which we try to provide a service that will add value to the world. It is therefore essential for us to look at our occupations as one of the main avenues and pillars of our life mission.

The first step to making your occupation part of your mission is picking the right one. The formula to deciding how you should spend the bulk of your days is dependent on four factors:

1. Strengths (what you are good at)
2. Passions (what you enjoy doing)
3. Impact (where you can make a difference)
4. Money (what your financial needs are)

This advice has become part of mainstream thought, and it has its roots in age-old Jewish teachings. In the classic work on personal growth, *Duties of the Heart*, the author writes:

Every person has a preference for a particular work or business over others. God has already implanted in his nature a love and fondness for it...Similarly, you will find among human beings character traits and body structures suited for certain businesses or activity. One who finds his nature and personality attracted to a certain occupation, and his body is suited for it, that he will be able to bear its demands—he should pursue it and make it his means of earning a livelihood, and he should bear its pleasures and pains and not be upset when sometimes his income is withheld. Rather, let him trust in God that He will support him all of his days.

STRENGTHS AND PASSIONS

We showed earlier that the very first question that we will be asked in the Next World is: "Did you conduct your work with *emunah* (lit., faith)?" *Emunah* can refer to being faithful to the people that you do business with, as well as having faith in God. But in addition to translating *emunah* as faith, we showed that the root of the word *emunah* is *omein*, an artisan or a craftsman.

What is the difference between someone that you would call an artisan, and just an everyday worker?

Workers have jobs. Artisans have crafts. Workers do what they have to do to get paid. Artisans, like artists, try to leave their mark on the world. An artisan is deeply connected to the work that they do because they are bringing their unique gifts to the world and bringing beauty from potential into actuality.

You don't have to be a painter, musician, glass blower, or knitter of hand-made sweaters from recyclable organic material to view your work as your piece of art. We are all artists and artisans. What is art, really? It is an individual's unique way of processing the world around them, interpreting what they see and feel and communicating that back into the world in a creative way. The way that you choose to process and communicate your gifts to the world is your art form, because only you can communicate with the world in that specific way.

When you see your occupation as more than just how you make your money or what you "have to do," but an avenue to use your skills and talents to make the world better—when you add your creative touch, your piece of you, your signature to whatever it is that you do—you are becoming an artisan. And it changes the way you will relate to your work and the way others will view your work as well.

Let's explore, however, what we really mean by strengths and passions. The very common advice to pursue your strengths and passions can be either an important guiding force in figuring out your path, or a big distraction. Motivational speakers will often throw out phrases such as "everyone has a superpower" or "you are put in this world to do the things that bring you joy" or "when you are doing what you are in this world to do, it will just feel right."

While there are certainly some people who have specific talents and passions that guide them exactly on the path that they need, this is not true for most people. The average person does not have one clear talent that is unmistakably and distinctly connected to their mission. And even those who have a special talent or passion can end up on a wild-goose chase to be someone that they are not meant to be, or on a fantasy road to nowhere when we overemphasize the role of talent. (Haven't you ever met someone who took a few guitar lessons and now believes that they are destined for the Rock and Roll Hall of Fame?) The reality is that not everyone who sounds good around the campfire is the next Jerry Garcia, and not everyone who can doodle is meant to be the next Rembrandt. The frustration of hearing that we should pursue our talents and then not feeling that our talents are enough can make us feel inferior about ourselves.

The reality is that whether or not we have one obvious talent that will guide us, every single person has a specific set of natural abilities and aptitudes that can be applied to guide them on their mission. It might be elements of their personality and nature such as their sense of humor, creativity, warmth and empathy, organizational skills, leadership traits, or the many other things that make us unique. An understanding of which of the four elements are our dominant ones will help us get started at identifying some of our strengths, such as the leadership skills of a dominant fire personality, the organizational skills of a dominant earth personality, the emotional awareness of a dominant water personality, and the intellectual ability or creativity of a dominant air personality.

But in addition to that, every aspect of one's unique personality is a window into what makes them unique and what they can bring to the world. Nothing should be discounted or shrugged off. No matter how simple or small you believe your unique traits are, those are going to be the tools that will help you on your journey. Every aspect of our personality, whether we believe that they are significant or not, can be used as a tool to make our mark in the world. The more we succeed at this, the more we will avail ourselves of one of the greatest joys and sense of fulfillment.

Many people tragically never fully express their special strengths and gifts to the world. There are many reasons for this. Some lack the self-confidence to believe that they can really make a difference. Some people never really recognize how gifted they are or suffer from "imposter syndrome," feeling inadequate to show off their talents since there are other people who can do it better. Others try and get discouraged when it doesn't work out at first. It is important to remember that whatever strengths you were given, no matter how big or small, they are there because God decided that for whatever you are here to do, this is a tool with which you can add your touch.

If you have some superstar talent, become a superstar. If you don't, you are no less valuable. If we are not the generals of the army, we can be soldiers. Soldiers are an absolute necessity in an army. You can't have an army where everyone is a general. The soldier who is playing his part faithfully is no less valuable than the general.

If talent cannot be directly turned into an occupation, it can often be used to enhance a person's occupation. Additionally, often the aptitudes that are behind this specific talent can be applied in other ways to contribute to successes in other areas.

A great example of this is when guiding students who struggle academically, but are great in sports. The majority of young people that are good at sports are not going to go pro, so we need to guide them how to channel those talents to make their impact. Being an athlete teaches kids so much about discipline, determination, and hard work. If they can approach the "game of life" with that same competitive mentality, they have the potential to win at whatever they do just by virtue of their ability to outwork and out-persevere their competitors.

This can be said about almost any talent or hobby. They are almost always windows into the person's deeper roots and can be very useful in getting a better understanding of what it is that can be applied to one's occupation.

IMPACT

It is very possible for a person to be doing what they are talented in and are passionate about and still not be accomplishing their mission. This is because their whole purpose in working is just about their own success, but is not at all focused on giving to others or making the world a better place. We discussed in chapter 8 the importance of viewing one's occupation as their way of serving others and transforming themselves into a giver. It is only through becoming a giver that we can really experience a truly satisfying career.

We see many gifted and talented people who are using their gifts and talents to become famous, rich, and powerful, yet they seem to be living very unfulfilled and shallow lives. When we learn about the lives of the rich and famous, we get the impression that many of them are feeling completely unfulfilled. Because they are using their talents, it may appear that they are doing what they were put in this world for, but unless they are using their gifts to make positive change, they are falling way short because they have not figured out how to properly channel their gifts.

There are definitely certain careers where it is easier to see how you are making a positive impact in the world and feel like that is part of your mission. Many people feel so connected to the work that they do that they will tell you about their jobs, "This is my life mission." Typically, people who say this have jobs that by their very nature provide a person with a tremendous amount of meaning and give them an opportunity to make the world a better place. This is true with many jobs in medicine, education, communal work, self-care, safety, etc.

But even those who have jobs that are not as fulfilling and it is not as obvious how they are making an impact, that doesn't mean that it is not also part of the bigger picture of one's mission. As we have said previously, one's life mission isn't necessarily always that glamorous. An army needs soldiers doing all types of work. Even jobs that are not necessarily all that glamorous might still put a person in a unique position to help someone or provide someone with a service that, for them, could be life-changing.

As we mentioned above, being masters of our craft requires more than just showing up to get paid and going home. We become masters of our craft when we figure out how to infuse our work with our creativity, our special touch, that shows that we really care about our work and the people who are affected by it. When we do that, we transform our job into our craft and begin to feel like this is indeed part of our mission in this world. The impact of this is felt by the people whom we work with and whom we work for, including employers and customers.

> WE BECOME MASTERS OF OUR CRAFT WHEN WE FIGURE OUT HOW TO INFUSE OUR WORK WITH OUR CREATIVITY, OUR SPECIAL TOUCH.

In recent years, many companies have outperformed their competitors by building a brand that is known to focus on relationships rather than just products. Some examples of this:

- Apple became the world's leading technology company by making the user-experience their top priority, while other companies were focused mainly on the technology.
- Large companies like Google and Zappos became famous for creating an internal culture that encourages their employees to feel like they are part of a family and therefore comfortable to try new things and be creative.
- The Magic Castle Hotel became L.A.'s fourth ranking hotel for some time simply because they invented the "Popsicle Hotline," where guests could order their favorite flavor popsicle while

they were sitting out at the pool and have it delivered by a waiter
wearing fancy white gloves.

It is this personal touch that causes buyers to pay tens of thousands
of dollars for clothes and accessories that are handmade, or why people
are willing to take lower salaries to work for certain companies. All of
these successes come from the fact that people appreciate when the
creator of a product or a service is thinking more about the people they
are affecting than the product they are creating.

This approach to one's work can be found in the Talmud as well. The
Talmud tells the story of Abba, the surgeon/bloodletter who earned
himself a ticket to spiritual greatness that included a daily greeting from
Heaven. This is because instead of just going about his daily business,
he figured out systems to perform his procedures with consideration for
the modesty of women and for the privacy of those who couldn't afford
to pay in full for his services. Simple acts of consideration for others
transformed a simple job into a craft worth Heavenly recognition.

Another expression of this is the midrashic account of the great
Biblical figure Hanoch, who was of angelic qualities. The midrash relates
that he was a shoemaker, and with every stitch that he would make on
the shoes he was making, he would be stitching together heaven and
earth. The commentators explain this to mean that he cared so deeply
for his customers that every stitch was done from a place of deep love
for them and to provide them with the highest quality work.[1]

This is the standard that we must adopt for our own work to transform it from a simple job to a craft that we are deeply connected to and
a part of our mission in this world.

MONEY

The need to support ourselves and our family is obviously going to be
a major consideration in how we decide to spend our days. The more financial responsibility or freedom that a person has will certainly affect
the type of occupation and specific job that a person undertakes.

---

1   Rabbi Yisrael Salanter, brought by Rabbi Eliyahu Dessler in *Strive for Truth*, vol. 1, essay
on Kindness.

When Adam and Eve were kicked out of Eden, God punished them with the words: "By the sweat of your brow shall you get bread to eat." This is both a curse and a blessing. On the one hand, much of the stress and anxiety in our life is revolved around providing for ourselves and our families. On the other hand, it does push us to be productive and innovative and stops us from becoming too lazy or complacent.

Though the financial aspect of our work is constantly on our mind, we are warned to make sure it doesn't come at the expense of doing an occupation that is not properly suited for us. We quoted above the words of the great author of the classic *Duties of the Heart* that "one who finds his nature and personality attracted to a certain occupation" should stick to it and "not be upset when sometimes his income is withheld."

While many people might be uncomfortable with the piece of advice given here, it is certainly something that we can observe to be true. I have met many people who had such a deep love for their craft that making money became secondary. They were more than happy to live with less for the privilege to do the job that they were doing. These folks exhibit a greater joy of life than anyone else that I know.

On the other hand, I have met many people who are trapped in "golden handcuffs." They find their work to be meaningless or boring, or they are unhappy with their job, yet remain there because of financial fear. This seems to be the responsible thing to do—and often, it is for some period of time—but in the long run, a person needs to find an occupation that will resonate inside of them as being a path that they were put into this world for. If you are miserable, I can assure you, that is not where you belong.

When we find ourselves in a job that doesn't properly utilize our skills, we are experiencing a taste of slavery. The commentaries teach us that this was one element of the slavery that the Jewish People experienced in Egypt. The Egyptians made sure that every individual engaged in tasks that would not allow them to express their talents and skills. They understood that the key to extinguishing a person's zest for life is to not allow them to achieve their potential.

The key to freedom is to realize our unique strengths, passions, and ability to impact others, and apply those to our occupation. Through our inner work on the four elements, we get to know and love ourselves and elevate our character. This then flows outward into the world, which can receive all of the positive energy that we have generated. We have become masters of our inner world and artists to the outer world.

But even then, our work is not done. We mentioned early on in our discussion that the purpose of self-mastery was to become vessels for an even higher and loftier experience. Now that we have a solid understanding of the four elements and how to apply them to impact the world, we have still another destination. Having looked inward and outward, we must turn our attention upward. In the next chapter, we will see what lies at the top of the inner ladder.

summary

We have seen the importance of approaching our occupations with creativity, and artisanship is key to accomplishing our mission in this world. Included in this is

- identifying one's unique strengths and passions—even the ones that do not seem too significant—and figuring out how to best apply them to one's occupation;
- using our unique and creative touch to transform our jobs into a way to impact people and become a giver;
- finding the correct balance between making money and finding a job that one truly enjoys.

18

THE TOP OF THE LADDER

He blew into him the breath of life,
and man became a living being.

Genesis 2:7

SPIRITUAL ACROPHOBIA

Acrophobia, also known as fear of heights, is one of the most common fears of human beings. When an acrophobe is standing on a high balcony or hiking on a tall mountain, they feel that they are only moments away from coming tumbling down to their imminent death.

In my observation, "spiritual acrophobia" is just as common. Many people have a fear of climbing too high on the ladder of personal growth for fear of failure or falling, or because they don't believe they can do it. Like the common acrophobe, they are fine as long as they have the lower rungs of the ladder to hold onto. But the moment that they think about what it will take to get to the top, the entire world starts to spin. In fact, studies have shown that when the common acrophobe is asked to assess the height of a tall object or building, they will almost always overestimate its size. This means that things seem higher, taller, and scarier than they actually are. The spiritual acrophobe is the same way, misjudging how close they really are to their greatest possible selves and how accessible it really is. But, in truth, it is much closer than one thinks.

We have seen that our inner world is like a ladder with its feet on the ground and its top in the heavens. In the previous chapters, we have shown how our entire life is a journey to self-mastery as we climb the inner ladder of our *nefesh* and reach for the higher levels of our soul. The higher we climb the ladder of our inner selves by becoming masters over the four inner elements, the more that we discover the greatness that resides inside of us. As we become the masters of our bodies, our emotions, our intellect, and our willpower, we transform ourselves to the way we were meant to be—the way Adam and Eve were created in the Garden of Eden.

We are then ready to reach the ultimate goal of all self-mastery—to have a more direct and sustained experience of our souls. We explained above that our higher Soul, or *Nefesh Elokis*, can be considered a fifth element waiting for us at the top of our inner ladder. This level of consciousness is what we referred to before as *daas* or *deveikus*, which is attachment or enlightenment. This unfamiliar destination that lies at the top of the ladder often seems beyond our grasp and is therefore frightening.

WHEN WE ENVISION THE TOP OF THE LADDER, RATHER THAN BEING AFRAID, WE SHOULD BE FILLED WITH THE JOY AND EXCITEMENT OF DISCOVERING THAT CLOSE AND CONSTANT CONNECTION.

The patriarch, Jacob, dreamt of a ladder reaching up until the heavens. The Kabbalists teach that this represents the inner ladder of the soul. Standing at the top of this ladder was God, Who said to him, "Remember, I am with you; I will protect you; I will not leave you."[1] When we envision the top of the ladder, rather than being afraid, we should be filled with the joy and excitement of discovering that close and constant connection. In this chapter, we will discuss how we can all climb just a little higher and reach up toward the top of the ladder.

---

1   Genesis 28:15.

LEVELS OF THE SOUL

How do you know you have a soul? What does it feel like? When do you feel it?

When I ask this question to my students, the answers usually vary. The most common answers include the following:

- "When I am out in the quiet of nature"
- "During meditation or prayer"
- "After I performed an act of kindness"
- "When I am around a very great person"
- "During intense physical movement"

Obviously, these are all vastly different experiences, each of which can be ascribed to different elements within us. But the one common denominator is that for every individual, there are certain moments when they discover a deeper part of themselves that seems greater and more spiritually connected than they are today. Any time a person has such an experience, it is priming them to become vessels for a much deeper, richer spiritual awareness.

But where do these sensations come from?

In order to really understand the soul experience and how it works, it is necessary for us to further define what the soul is and where is resides. We quoted the great Kabbalist and philosopher Rabbi Moshe Chaim Luzzatto as describing the soul "as having many parts that are bound to each other like links on a chain. Each of these are bound to the one below it until the lowest one is bound to the animal soul, which in turn is linked to the blood, and that is where the body and soul meet."[2]

Let's define what those different links are. Just as our lower *nefesh* has four elements, the higher soul is also built of four different parts. Since the soul is considered the "breath of God,"[3] their names are all reflections of the breathing process. They are called:

- *Nefesh* (the destination and resting place of the breath)
- *Ruach* (the breath in motion)

---

2   *The Way of God* 3:1.
3   Genesis 2:7.

- *Neshamah* (the breath when it is still in the realm of the blower)
- *Chayah* (the source of the breath)

Each one of these levels of the higher soul corresponds to the different domains in the lower soul:

- *Nefesh* to the body
- *Ruach* to the emotions
- *Neshamah* to the mind
- *Chayah* to the willpower

And just as the four elements of the lower soul are greeted at the top by the higher soul, the four levels of the higher soul are also rooted in an even higher level called *yechidah*. The root of this is *echad*, one, because at this level, the soul is at one with its Divine source.

As we climb the ladder of self-mastery, our lower soul becomes a vessel for the higher soul, which can then be experienced through the other faculties:

- The *nefesh* level gives us an awareness and an identification of our spiritual souls as the true "I." Our bodies feel like nothing more than a vehicle for our soul but not as who we really are.
- The *ruach* attaches and expresses itself through our emotions and is experienced as a powerful emotional awakening of our spirit. At its highest level, *ruach* is experienced as a complete transcendence and ecstasy, known in Kabbalistic works as *ruach hakodesh*.
- The *neshamah* level attaches and expresses itself through the realm of thought, giving man the ability to know and understand purely spiritual and holy truths.
- The highest level, *chayah*, is connected to the realm of will, and though it is so powerful that it is beyond direct experience, we are connected to it and draw from it, like an electrical appliance that draws electricity from the wires that are outside of it.

SOUL SEARCHING

Mastery over any of the four elements doesn't happen all at once. Despite Hollywood's portrayal of "falling in love," which happens instantaneously and with dramatic music in the background, we know that developing deep love is a slow process. It comes on early as a strong emotion, then waxes and wanes and reinvents itself as something more permanent. Intellectual clarity acts in the very same way. We have an "aha!" moment, then uncertainty, then finally our thoughts seem to settle. The power of will creates a fire inside of us, then cools, and that reignites as a steady flame inside of us.

The spiritual experience occurs in the very same manner. It isn't instantaneous. It comes and goes—sometimes as big waves and sometimes as subtle undertones. Then it fades, leaving just a residue. Each time it comes and goes, however, it leaves just a little more of itself behind until slowly, slowly, over a long period of time, we have developed a greater spiritual awareness, arriving at the top of the ladder without ever really fully knowing when or how it happened.

There is a profound Biblical story about the prophet Elijah, who is trying to experience the Divine. He has a whole series of very loud and dramatic sensations, but none of those are God. But then he experiences something very quiet and realizes that that is exactly what he was looking for:

> *There was a great and mighty wind, splitting mountains, and shattering rocks by the power of Hashem (God); but Hashem was not in the wind. After the wind—an earthquake; but Hashem was not in the earthquake. After the earthquake—fire; but Hashem was not in the fire. And after the fire—a soft whispering voice.*[4]

It is this soft whispering voice that we need to be listening out for as we go through our daily lives. Our entire life-mission is to search for it like one who lost an unbelievably valuable object and cannot rest until it is found.

We mentioned earlier that our Sages teach us that Adam and Eve reached from "one end of the world to the other." This means that their

---

4   I Kings 19:11–12.

consciousness reached the highest possible levels. But this is not the only time that our Sages speak about the great potential of human consciousness. If Adam and Eve seem very distant from you, you should know that the experience is a lot closer than you think.

Our Sages describe the scene in heaven at the moment that a child is conceived. The Almighty summons the soul that is destined to come into the world and gives it its unique qualities. They describe how before the child enters into the world, "A light burns above its head and it looks and sees from *one end of the world to the other*."[5] This state is almost identical to that of Adam and Eve in the Garden of Eden. But right before we enter the world, "an angel approaches, strikes its mouth, and causes it to forget."

The Talmud is telling us something fascinating. Before we come into this world, our soul is taught the whole Torah and shown everything that we need to know to accomplish our mission in the world. But at the moment we are about to enter the world, the angel taps us right above our lip, and we forget it all. What is the point of teaching it all to us if we are just going to forget it?

The forgetting that we are speaking about here doesn't mean that it is completely erased from our memory. It means that it is driven deep into our subconscious so that we will have to search for it on our own as we go through life. But whenever we encounter an experience that reminds of what our soul felt, it awakens a place deep inside of us; it feels right; it excites us! And it is true vice versa as well. When we neglect pursuing our mission, when we are traveling down roads that lead us away from what we know deep down in our soul, we begin to feel empty and void, we begin to thirst for more and yearn to reconnect to our inner roots.

HABITS OF SOUL SEEKERS

LISTEN INWARD

Throughout our life, we must pay close attention to the inner voice of our soul that is calling out to us and trying to remind us that it is

---

5   Talmud, *Niddah* 30b.

there. When life is so fast-paced and busy, it becomes very hard to hear the whisper over all of the noise. We need to carve out time in our life to stop and listen and allow ourselves to reconnect to that higher place that is inside of us.

This can happen during a long walk in nature, during meditation, or even through powerful music. In fact, we know that many prophets used music to awaken feelings of joy and try to enter into higher states of consciousness.[6] The commonality of all of those practices is that they fully align all of our inner domains, creating harmony and synergy between them. The body, earth element, becomes weightless and energetic. The emotion, water level, becomes full of love and openness. The mind, wind element, becomes clear and calm. And the will, fire element, becomes ignited and alive. When all is aligned, we have now made ourselves vessels for our soul to whisper to us. When that happens, we want to lean into that moment as much as we can. It might come and go, but it will make a lasting impact.

Rabbi Klonymous Kalman Shapira, also known as the Rebbi of Piascezna, says that at those very moments when one is feeling inspired and spiritually connected, one should try to either say a prayer, think about a Torah insight, or do a kind act, in order to do something to crystallize that feeling.[7] At the very least, it would help to write down what a person is feeling at that moment to try to capture it in some way.

PRAYER

Jewish prayer is meant to be one of the main avenues that we use to awaken the still voice that is inside of us. By taking some time away from the daily bustle, we try to loosen the bonds between our souls and our bodies and raise our consciousness. The words serve as mantras and tools to channel our thoughts and emotions upward. This is why repetition of the same words is so essential. The familiarity with the words allows us to focus less on the meaning of the words themselves

---

6   II Kings 3:15.
7   *Hachsharas Ha'Avreichim.*

and to lean into the cumulative feelings and emotions that we associate with those words.

So the more one prays, the more the words serve as a launching pad for a higher experience. The words become the vehicle, and the feeling of connection is the clear destination. Different lines in prayer speak to different people so that every individual ends up developing their own "highlight reel" of lines in prayer that excites them.

THE MORE ONE PRAYS, THE MORE THE WORDS SERVE AS A LAUNCHING PAD FOR A HIGHER EXPERIENCE.

When we pray, we try to engage every level of ourselves: the swaying of our bodies engages our earth element; the expressions of joy and love that are woven throughout many of the prayers engage our element of water; the words that we speak engage our wind element; and the yearning for God is meant to engage our element of fire.

The more we can quiet down our minds before we enter into prayer, the richer the experience that we will have. This is why the Talmud teaches that pious people would meditate for an hour before they would pray.[8] Often, the first few minutes of prayer are the most difficult because it takes some time for our minds to get settled. Instead of quieting down, the mind becomes flooded with all of the different thoughts that have been swimming around and waiting for our attention. If we stay on course and gracefully channel our attention back to spiritual thoughts and feelings, we eventually become "locked-in" and into a state of flow. The problem is that often the rush of thoughts into our heads as we begin to pray derails us, and we throw in the towel without ever fully connecting.

SHABBAT

Shabbat is a great time to try to generate such soul experiences, as it is a time of absolute renewal for our inner world. More and more, experts in top performance and human potential from all walks of life are realizing the importance of having time to recharge and refresh, and

---

8   Talmud, *Berachos* 30b.

Shabbat awards us the time for just that! Unplugging for an extended period of time provides us a space to quiet down the hustle of our lives.

Just as the six days of creation were a time when the Almighty was creating a world of elements with the final step of creation, Day seven, focusing on the spiritual component of the world, we also have the ability to transcend our elemental levels on Shabbat and access our spiritual realms. Just as Shabbat is a day of being, and not a day of doing, our soul, as well, is experienced when we are in a state of being, completely present, rather than when we are frantically coming and going. Although Adam and Eve fell from their lofty levels on the Friday that they were created, they were not sent out of Eden until after Shabbat. This is because Shabbat provides a space for even those who are struggling to taste Eden.

Shabbat engages all of our inner elements: the earth element is reenergized by the slowing down and resting; the water element is elevated by the pleasures of the delicious food and quality time with one's loved ones; the time to think, read, and converse gives expression to the wind element; and a holy fire is reignited when we have the space to step back from our constant productivity, goals, and ambitions to remind ourselves that God is in charge.[9]

summary

We have seen how through mastery of the four inner elements, we become vessels to experience our souls and reach a state of consciousness called *daas* or *deveikus*. The soul itself has many levels that can be attained as we grow in our spirituality. There are different practices that we can do to become more aware of our souls, including

---

9   We saw above that the way to elevate the element of fire is through awe of God. We quoted the Talmud that says, "The Holy One, blessed be He, has nothing in his treasury other than a treasure of awe of Heaven." Interestingly, the Talmud elsewhere teaches us that there is actually something else in God's treasury: "God said to Moses, 'I have a wonderful gift in My storehouse named Shabbat, and I wish to give it to Yisrael.'" Clearly, we see that Shabbat is a time that is auspicious for developing this trait. It is also noteworthy that awe of God is the seventh question on the list of post-life questions, just as Shabbat is the seventh day and a day that we are meant to grow spiritually.

- engaging in activities that quiet down one's state of mind during a long walk in nature, during meditation, or through music, and then trying to fill the quiet space with a spiritual thought or act;
- heartfelt prayer that comes from a quiet mind, specifically by the repetition of lines that one finds inspiring;
- using Shabbat as a time to elevate each of the four inner elements.

19

HOW TO MAKE REAL CHANGE

Know where you are coming from,
and where you are going.

Ethics of Our Fathers 3:1

TAKING ACTION

Ten frogs are sitting on a log. Nine decide to jump off. How many are left?

Sounds easy, right? But before you decide on your answer, let me tell you that this riddle is a favorite among many influencers and performance coaches. Because anyone in the business of trying to influence change in others knows that motivating someone to want to change is only the very first step in actually creating change. Most people who attend seminars, read self-help books, and spend thousands of dollars on courses essentially change very little. This is because they never develop a real plan for how to change.

The answer to the riddle is that there are still ten frogs on the log because nine of them only "decided" to jump, and a decision without taking action is worth nothing.

We have gone through the various steps that are necessary to accomplish one's mission in this world, but just reading about it without taking action will leave us in a place no different than the one that we are in today. Even when we take action, it won't happen overnight. But we need to put ourselves on a course of action to maximize our time and keep moving forward. With the proper plan of action, we are certainly capable of making massive strides. In this chapter, we are going to do just that. We are going to explore time-tested methods to create a plan of action and make real long-lasting change.

So, let's explore these methods and steps.

STEP 1: VISUALIZING THE IDEAL YOU

Close your eyes. Using the four-elements model as your inspiration, imagine yourself as being your very best self. You have mastered all the elements inside of you and are the king of all of your inner domains. Until now, we have been speaking about great Biblical personalities, but now we are looking at the ideal you. Try to visualize this ideal "you" in different scenarios: at home, at work, in the morning, in the evenings, with your family, and by yourself.

We are not talking here about things that you would like to accomplish. We are talking about who you want to *be*. How you want to show up every day for yourself and for the people around you. Visualize this until you have reached a point where you completely adore this ideal you. Think about how you would describe this version of yourself. Think about how others would describe this version. (Consider writing down on a paper a description of this version of yourself that you visualized.)

Visualize how you have mastered the earth element and are now constantly full of energy and joy. You maximize your time, moving with zeal from one task to the next. You have set routines and habits that you are proud of, including a morning routine that sets up your day for success. You live with an abundance mindset so that you can give of yourself and your resources generously and rejoice in other people's success.

Visualize how you have mastered the water element and know how to get the highest forms of pleasure out of life. You have deep relationships with others and a close-knit circle of loved ones whom you can pour your heart into. You are no longer enticed by the simplistic or addictive pleasures because you have discovered what really gives you true pleasure.

Visualize how you have mastered the wind element and are becoming wiser and wiser each day. You have become a lifelong learner, always excited to uncover more depth, more truth, and more of the amazing secrets that the universe is holding. Your conversations are meaningful, productive, and positive, and you are surrounded by like-minded people who don't just accept life at face value.

Visualize how you have mastered the fire element and live life fearlessly and humbly. You are always looking for new ways to fulfill your potential and self-actualize, and you are an inspiration to others. The people around you look up to you for your leadership, and you know how to empower them and bring out the best in them.

Visualize how you are spending your days involved in projects that bring out your strengths and passions, impacting other people in your unique way, and making money in the process.

Visualize how you have become deeply aware of your soul and plugged in to your inner world. You can freely disconnect from the fast pace of the external world and connect deeply to that place inside of you that is filled with holiness and bliss. You live with constant spiritual awareness and feel that your relationship with the Almighty is real and passionate.

Now, before you continue, ask yourself: How big was the gap between the person that you visualized and the person that you are today?

For this journey to be exciting enough to actually stick to it, there must be a significant enough gap between the reality of today and the ideal that we are trying to reach. Going from good to very good is not very enticing. Going from good to great—now that is exciting! There needs to be a bit of a stretch. It needs to present a significant enough challenge that when we get there, we are going to be proud of ourselves. That being said, if it is too much of a stretch that we don't really believe that we can accomplish it, it won't be taken seriously and won't meet success.

Finally, to ensure that you have created an exciting enough image for yourself, you need to ask yourself one more question: Is it worth the pain necessary to get there? Think about what costs this journey might incur, what obstacles one might face, and what the difficulties are that are going to be a result of going on this path. Is this vision really worth all that pain? If you can't confidently say that it is, it is likely that this vision of yourself won't motivate you that much later on down the road. Either dig deeper and articulate the benefits of the journey or pick a direction that has a bigger payoff.

So, when you visualize this version of yourself, ask yourself these four questions:

1. Does it excite you?
2. Will it be a stretch to get there?
3. Do you believe that it is possible?
4. Is it worth the pain?

STEP 2: BREAKING IT DOWN

We mentioned above that depending on your inner wiring, you might find that you have naturally mastered some of the attributes discussed throughout this book but need some or a lot of work in others. Based on the image of the ideal you that you have created, create a list of traits that you are inspired to work on. The list can be as long or short as you would like.

Try to write all of the things that you would like to work on in the form of positive traits that you would like to master, rather than things that you would like to stop doing. So, while it might come naturally to write things like "not speak gossip," "not waste time," or "not lose my temper," realize that showing restraint or "not doing" is so much harder and much less exciting than "doing," i.e., taking proactive steps to overcoming a negative trait. So, replace "not speak gossip" with "always speak positively." Instead of "not waste time," try "find more productive ways to relax." And in place of "not lose my temper," how about "become a calm and happy person, even in very stressful situations."

Next to each trait that you would like to master, identify what element this trait is rooted in, to the best of your understanding. It could be either a positive or negative trait that is rooted in earth, water, wind, or fire:

- If you feel that it relates to your physical body, productivity, or mood, connect it to earth.
- If you feel it has to do with pleasure, emotions, or close relationships, connect it to water.
- If you feel it is connected to how you communicate, your intellect, creativity, or your thinking process, connect it to wind.
- And if it has to do with motivation, determination, or humility, connect it to the fire element.

There are a few benefits to connecting it to an element:

1. **Self-awareness**—If we find that several of the traits that we want to work on are heavily concentrated on one or two of the elements, that is a clear indication for us about how we are wired and where we need to put in a bulk of our efforts. It also might make us aware of other traits that are connected to that element that perhaps we didn't realize was a struggle for us.

2. **Simplicity**—Seeing a whole list of things that we need to work on can be overwhelming and discouraging. However, when we see the traits grouped together, it is more reassuring and seems more manageable. We can assume that as we work on one trait, we are elevating that inner element, and other traits will be affected as well. For example, working on "becoming a more positive person" and "waking up earlier in the morning" might seem like two different tasks. That is overwhelming. But when we group both of those things under the earth element, we become hopeful that as we work on one, the other will organically become easier to work on.

3. **Scheduling**—Grouping traits by their elements will also help us in scheduling when we work on it, as we will see in the coming step.

STEP #3—CREATING A SCHEDULE

One of the most common reasons that people are not successful in working on their character traits is because they are focusing on too many things at once. The great masters of personal growth advise against this, as well as working on one thing for too long. So, what we need to do now is to create a system of when we will be focusing on which traits.

The length and frequency of how much we work on each trait are very much subjective. The purpose, though, is that during a set amount of time, you will be hyper-focused on this trait, using the tools that will be described further. After that, it is best to move on to other traits for a set period of time and come back to each one at a later date. It was common among the masters of personal develovement to create a cycle of thirteen traits. This way they could spend one week devoted to each trait and get to it four times a year.

One very meaningful and effective system to use relates very much to our approach up until now. That is to set aside specific months to work on traits that are related to the element that they are rooted in. So, you will have a month of working on earth-related traits, a month on water-related traits, and so on. You can work on one to two traits at a time for 1–2 weeks, but all within the framework of the element of that month.

In addition to this creating consistency, there are other benefits to using this system as well. Kabbalistic tradition teaches that certain months are auspicious to work on certain traits that relate to different elements (note: this system is working with the Jewish months, which are based on the lunar calendar). The relationship between a month and its element is connected to many factors, such as the zodiac symbol of that month, the holidays that fall out during that month, the Torah portions that we read during that month, or the Biblical events that happened during that month. Their calendar looks like this:

(A full explanation of the connection is beyond the scope of this book, but here are just a few small connections to better understand how they are connected.)

Nissan—fire	The month that the Jewish People left Egypt is a month of beginnings and making bold moves, which are connected to the element of fire. Passover was celebrated in the Holy Temple with the Pascal sacrifice, which would be roasted in fire. It was the month that Jewish kings would count the beginning of their reign, as fire symbolizes humble leadership.
Iyar—earth	The month is marked by the counting of the Omer, a system of steady, consistent, and incremental growth until the receiving of the Torah in the following month. Consistent hard work is represented by the earth element.
Sivan—air	This is the month that the Jewish People received the Torah and its laws. The element of air is connected with study, analyzing, and expanding one's mind.
Tamuz—water	Tamuz is considered a sad month in the Jewish calendar because of several tragic events that happened during that month. In this month, the Jewish People served the golden calf after receiving the Torah. It is therefore appropriate to work on overcoming some of the negative traits that cause a person to fall. The element of water is connected to lust and temptation. The zodiac sign for Tamuz is cancer, with its symbol as the crab, a water creature, and is connected to emotions and temptations.
Av—fire	This is also considered a sad month as it is the month when the Temple was destroyed. The image of the burning flames of destruction are connected to the fire element. The Temple was destroyed because of how people mistreated each other, which, as we spoke about the people of Sodom, is connected to fire. The zodiac sign for this month is Leo, the lion, which is a symbol of great leadership, and in Jewish tradition great kings are born in Av.
Elul—earth	This month begins the preparation and hard work to get ready for Rosh Hashanah and Yom Kippur, and because of that it is similar to the month of Iyar that we mentioned earlier, which is connected to the element of earth and requires detailed, consistent growth.
Tishrei—air	This is the month of Rosh Hashanah, Yom Kippur, and Sukkos. It is also when the Jewish People received the Torah for the second time after they served the golden calf. As we said with the month of Sivan, the deep study and analysis of the Torah is represented by the air element.
Cheshvan—water	This month is the beginning of the rainy season in Israel, so it is connected to water. It is also the month that Noah's flood occurred, in which, as we spoke about earlier, was the repercussion of the temptations that the generation was guilty of.
Kislev—fire	The month that Chanukah falls in is represented by the flames of the Menorah and the great leadership and bravery of the Maccabees in the struggle against the Greeks during the times of the Second Temple.

Teves—earth	This month comes at the heart of the cold and dark winter. It is also considered the third sad month and contains a fast day for the siege on Jerusalem. The dark symbolism of this month is connected to the struggles of the element of earth, which is sadness and sluggishness.
Shevat—air	This month contains Tu B'Shevat, which is a celebration of the blossoming of trees in Israel and the beginning of renewal. It was in this month that the entire last book of the Torah, Moses's last will and testament, was said. It is therefore considered a month of creativity and individuality, which is connected to the air element. Its zodiac sign is Aquarius, which is associated with free-spirited and creative thinking.
Adar—water	The final month is when the Purim story happened. The shape-shifting nature of water is connected to the Purim story, which was about the great turnabout of events in Persia, and is why we celebrate Purim by putting on masks and disguising ourselves. Water is also connected to the zodiac sign of Adar, which is Pisces, fish.

STEP #4—WORKING ON OUR CHARACTER TRAITS

During the time that you designate to work on this trait, make sure that you are doing daily work to ensure that you will make progress. Designate about twenty minutes every morning and every evening to "do the work." The goal of all of this work is to create as much awareness in your mind as possible that will last throughout the day. The greatest challenge to change is that our brain operates on habit. The more that we engage in the following exercises, we create new neurological pathways in our brain that disrupt the patterns that create habits.

While much has been written about the power of habit in the general world in recent years, we find that it was written about and recommended as part of Jewish tradition for centuries. In the book *Cheshbon Hanefesh* (an accounting of the soul), which deals with how to break habits, the author writes:

> *Every single feeling, no matter how small it is, and even if it is forgotten by the conscious mind, always leaves some sort of impression on the memory. If one then experiences this feeling a second time, it combines with the original impression, thereby strengthening itself. Every time this feeling is experienced again, all the accumulated traces of the previous*

impressions combine with it. Over time, the most insignificant string of experiences can accumulate to become strong enough to overwhelm even a major experience.[1]

In order to create constant awareness of whatever trait we are working on, follow the following five steps:

DAILY STUDY/READING

Prepare a series of material to study throughout the week that is related to the trait you are working on. It should include some reading material, such as a book or a series of articles. Other media such as videos, audio, and podcasts are great as well. Whatever you are working on, there is no shortage of material on that trait. Each day, spend a few minutes each morning and evening reading those texts that are related to your trait of the week.

JOURNALING

Create a journal notebook that you write in each morning and evening. As you go through those texts, take note of the ideas that are specifically powerful and write them down in the journal, especially sentences or phrases that resonate deeply with you. Each morning, think about the day and write down two or three goals for that specific day. In the evening, jot down a few short lines about how you did that day with accomplishing your goals. It can be something as simple as a check or an X. The point is that when you are in the routine of writing it down, it will be in the back of your mind the entire day.

VISUALIZATIONS

In the morning, as you are writing down in the journal your goals for the day, close your eyes and actually visualize yourself going through the scenario and being the person that you would like to be. Imagine yourself winning and being perfect. This will create new patterns in your brain that are just as powerful as the habit that you are trying to get rid of. This practice was first brought to the public eye in the world

---

1   *Cheshbon Hanefesh* §53.

of sports, when it was discovered that athletes who spend time creating an image in their mind of them being successful in their sport actually outperformed their competitors.[2] Their mental practice had a powerful effect on their performance because they had properly trained their brain to function in a certain way. The power of visualization was so effective that people started practicing it in their daily life. They would spend time envisioning how the day would go, how they would close the deal, how they would respond in a certain situation, and it showed to have a massive effect on people's life.

This practice, too, has been found in Jewish writing for centuries. Consider this a quote from the last will and testament of the great spiritual master Rebbe Elimelech of Lizhensk, known as the Noam Elimelech:

> *When you are idle in a room by yourself or lying in bed unable to sleep, concentrate on sanctifying God's Name…God counts a thought as a deed, and as a result you are not idly sitting or lying but fulfilling a commandment in the Torah.*

AFFIRMATIONS/MANTRAS

Take some of your favorite and most powerful quotes from your studying and turn it into your affirmation or your "mantra" for the day. (For example, if you are working on self-esteem, you might want to take the famous phrase from our Sages, "The world was created for me."[3]) Create constant reminders of your mantra by printing it out and hanging it on your refrigerator or a wall that you constantly stare at or pass by. Set it on your phone to pop up throughout the day. Anything else that you can do to have these lines become front and center will help you stay aware of this. The great masters of personal development would do an exercise called *hispa'alus*, which means "call to action," where they would repeat the phrase again and again, maybe in a chant or sing-song type way. If your mantra happens to be the lyrics of a catchy song, try

---

2   Tim Gallwey, *The Inner Game of Tennis.*
3   *Sanhedrin* 37a.

to hum that song throughout the day. If not, become a song-writer and write your own. Don't worry, nobody's listening.

REWARD YOURSELF

Everyone can use a little accountability as well as an extra incentive. Challenge yourself. When you hit a certain amount of victories, treat yourself to something special. Buy yourself your favorite dinner, or something new that you have been pushing off buying, or a new car! Whatever is your thing, spoil yourself with a reward!

Finally, at the end of the period of focused growth, reflect back on the time that you spent on this trait and ask yourself if there are any routines that you picked up that you will want to try to continue in order to maintain the new habit. So, for example, if you were working on the trait of alacrity and you consistently woke up a half an hour earlier every single day, it might not be in your best interest to just go back to sleeping late. Ask yourself if it is feasible for you to continue this pattern; if not, can you at least make a compromise and only move it up fifteen minutes instead of the full half an hour?

Remember that change doesn't happen overnight. We are not supposed to be perfect. Self-mastery means that you are in a constant state of improvement and working on yourself. If you consistently follow these steps, then you will find that over time things that were difficult at first will become habit, and slowly you will see how you have become a master of your inner world.

summary

We have seen the importance of creating a plan of action if we are serious about accomplishing our mission. The steps to do so are as follows:

1. Visualize the ideal You.
2. Break it down into specific traits and the elements that they are connected to.
3. Create a schedule of when you will work on what.
4. Do the work that includes (1) studying, (2) journaling, (3) visualization, (4) mantras, (5) rewards, and (6) takeaways.

20

YOUR BIG MOMENT

There is no man who doesn't have his hour.

Ethics of Our Fathers 4:3

THE GREAT SPIRITUAL MASTER known as the Baal Shem Tov would say: "A soul comes down for 70–80 years just to do a favor for someone else." Imagine that! A whole life lived just for one experience, one interaction, one moment.

Over the course of this book, we have outlined a very thorough plan for living a life of greatness. It involves a very high level of self-mastery by elevating the four elements and climbing one's inner ladder to reach our highest level of consciousness. It involves turning your occupation into a craft that you are passionate about and making your impact in this world. And it requires creating a plan of action that you will consistently stick to.

YOUR MISSION IN THIS WORLD COMES DOWN TO MOMENTS OF GREATNESS But all said and done, your mission in this world comes down to moments of greatness. Our Sages emphasize this point many times teaching us that "There is no man who doesn't have his hour,"[1] and "One moment of returning to God or doing good for

---

1   *Ethics of Our Fathers* 4:3.

someone else in this world is better than all of paradise."[2] The Rabbis of the Talmud echo this point as well by teaching us that despite the fact that a person can live an entire life going down the wrong path and immersed in pursuits that are the antitheses of a meaningful life, "there are those who acquire their place in the Next World in one small moment."[3]

This point is powerfully illustrated in the story surrounding the holiday of Purim found in the Book of Esther. Esther was an orphan girl who never knew her parents but became the queen to the most powerful king in the world.

When the Jews are under threat of annihilation, her cousin Mordechai sends her a message to go to the king and plead on behalf of the Jewish People, even though doing so could result in her death. Mordechai responds, "Who knows? Perhaps it is for this very moment that God put you in this position of royalty."

These words cry out to us in many situations in our life when we are put in a position when we can make a difference. They are words that should be circling in our head all of the time. Who knows? Maybe this whole trip into this world, maybe my whole destiny, is somehow dependent on this moment.

STOP WAITING FOR A BIG MOMENT!

When we view the world through this lens, every moment of our life has the potential to become that "big" moment. When we are together with people, we see new possibilities of how we can affect them. When we are all alone, we see new opportunities to look inward and work on ourselves. When we are in a joyful or spiritually high place, we can grab the chance to revel in our expanded consciousness; and when we are experiencing a low point or an internal battle, we seize the opportunity to acquire small victories in our pursuit of self-mastery. Our entire life becomes a symphony of these powerful moments.

---

2   Ibid. 4:17.
3   Talmud, *Avodah Zarah* 17a.

Many people never fully live because they are waiting around for something to happen:

- The next job is going to be my dream job.
- Things will settle down soon, and then I will make time for the important things.
- Pretty soon I will be ready to start a family.
- Pretty soon I'll get off the couch and in shape.

And the list goes on.

Those who live life to the fullest are those who realize that every single day is part of the journey and is bringing them closer to accomplishing their mission. Sometimes it feels big and sometimes it feels small. But if we did even one small thing every single day with the specific intention to become great, those efforts will compound and snowball and exponentially affect our growth.

In many ways, we can compare our personal growth to compound interest. Stock investors knows the power of compound interest. A little money that you invest today that continues to be reinvested again and again will slowly grow and grow into a figure that completely overshadows the original investment. But aside from teaching us how to become millionaires, compound interest also teaches us a wonderful lesson in personal growth: consistency.

A very famous anecdote is told of a billionaire lying on his deathbed who summons his two sons to share with them his final will and testament. When discussing how he will allocate his fortunes, he gives each one a choice. One option is to take home that very day one million dollars cash. The other is to earn a penny that day, and as long as they don't take home the penny, it will double its value on the next day. This can continue for up to thirty days so that for each day that the son decides to leave the money in the father's estate, the full value of the money will double.

The older son immediately jumps to take the million dollars. He doesn't want to play any games or take any chances. "How much can a penny grow in thirty days?" he thinks. The younger son, though, looks into his father's eyes and understands that his father is communicating something very important. He chooses the penny.

On the second day, the younger son's penny became worth two cents. On the third day, four cents. Then eight cents. Then sixteen. The younger brother checks in every now and then and begins to question whether this was a good idea. But on day thirty, when the brothers meet up, they decide to compare their fortunes. The older brother's million is still a million, but the younger brother's fortune has grown to over five million dollars!

This very same lesson can be applied to our growth. There will definitely be people whom we encounter who are propelled to "greatness" in a short period of time. Maybe a door will open for them, and they will find themselves in the limelight or with a very clear path. But for most of us, it is a daily grind. It is a constant investment and reinvestment of ourselves that slowly, slowly produces results.

Like the hour hand on a clock, we don't ever clearly see it moving, even if we don't take our eyes off of it. But one cannot argue that at the end of the hour it isn't in a different place than where it started.

One of the great spiritual giants of Judaism would often tell his students that they can become great in five minutes. When the students would express their bewilderment, he would tell them:

> *You become great by how you use the extra five minutes that you have periodically. If when you have an extra five minutes you decide to waste them, you will live a life of mediocrity. But if you realize that all of those extra five minutes can be used to start accomplishing something great, and then continue next time you have five minutes and then again next time. Then you will truly achieve greatness.*

This is the rule of compound self-growth in action.

Even a quiet moment in the privacy of one's home can turn into a powerful growth experience. We discussed earlier in the book (chapter 19) the power of visualizations and how we can actually change how our brains operate just by creating strong imagery in our minds about how we want to act and feel. Since our mind really never stops thinking, that means that every moment we are either improving as a human being or sliding backward. Every moment becomes an opportunity for growth if we learn how to channel that power. As we mentioned above from the great Chassidic master, the Noam Elimelech: "At every moment...when you are idle in a room by yourself or lying in bed unable to sleep, concentrate on sanctifying God's name...God will count these thoughts as a deed."

When we see the value of every moment this way, we become real connoisseurs of life. We start valuing every moment and every experience more and more. Every interaction, every word, and every smile become valuable. Our life becomes qualitatively different.

Consider the following story that is told about the great artist Picasso. He was sitting in a restaurant doodling on a napkin. A fellow nearby noticed the great artist, approached him, and offered to buy the doodled napkin. Picasso responded that he would be happy to sell it for 10,000 dollars. The man was astonished at the exorbitant price.

"It took you only five minutes to doodle that picture!" the potential buyer exclaimed.

"You are right," responded the artist. "But it took me my whole life to become Picasso."

You are an artist! Every moment of your life is valuable. Every experience, every high, and every low has made you into the person that you are today. You are here to continue to create your art and to beautify the world in a way that only you can. And when you are doing that, every single moment becomes priceless.

summary

In this chapter, we emphasized the value of every moment and how our mission can come down to specific moments and instances in our life. We therefore need to look at every moment in our life through the lens that this could perhaps be our big moment!

CONCLUSION
LECH LECHA: THE JOURNEY BEGINS!

*The two most important moments of your
life are the day that you are born and the
day that you find out why.*

Mark Twain

WHEN WE WERE YOUNG, we dreamed of greatness. We would travel the world and to outer space, become world-famous entertainers, great spiritual leaders, win Olympic gold medals, become the president, an NFL quarterback or, at the very least, Mashiach (Messiah). And then the grind of real life and (perhaps) some disappointment hit, and maybe we became content with being just "regular" people.

We are all destined for greatness. But without the proper definition of greatness, we might find ourselves dreaming of a path that is not appropriate for us and getting frustrated in the process. In the chapters of this book, we defined what greatness means for each of us—by looking inward, outward, and upward, and coming to the realization that everything that is in our life is part of our mission. We have been chosen to be placed in the exact circumstances that we find ourselves in because this is exactly where our mission lies. The journey to greatness begins right where you are standing.

The very first spiritual quest that the Torah takes us on is the quest of Abraham and Sarah. As we saw, that was the beginning of the process to repair the damage done to the four inner elements. Their journey begins with the very famous words spoken by God, the very precious statement that began the entire journey that led to the development of the Jewish nation:

> *Lech Lecha (go forth) from your native land and from your father's house to the land that I will show you.*[1]

Abraham was in his mid-seventies and Sarah in her mid-sixties when they began on this journey. They were not youngsters. At this point in their lives, they had already led a mass movement of change in the world, with thousands of students flocking to learn from them. But at that point in their life, a new journey begins with a vague description of "to the land that I will show you" as their final destination.

In Jewish tradition, everything that happens in our ancestral heritage is meant to symbolize patterns that are embedded in all of our stories. Whether you are celebrating your Bar/Bat Mitzvah or your great-grandchild's Bar/Bat Mitzvah, the Almighty is calling out to you to "go forth" and begin a new journey today!

The journey of Abraham and Sarah was not always a smooth one. Our Sages teach us that Abraham and Sarah were tested ten times on that journey.[2] Each time was another bump in the road to see whether they would stay on course. And they did. And that, too, is part of our story.

Perhaps we have experienced this in our own life. We have begun a new project, a new job, a new relationship, a new home, with such clarity that this is right for us, that this is where success will be found. And after making a shift in our life to accommodate this new endeavor and invest ourselves in it, often to the point of no return, we suddenly hit a wall. The clarity, the excitement, and the feelings of hope are gone. We are shocked that the project that gave us so much satisfaction now seems empty. That the person who seemed so perfect now seems so flawed. The job that was our dream is so frustrating.

---

1   Genesis 12:1.
2   *Ethics of Our Fathers* 5:3.

For so many, these are the moments in their life when they are ready to throw in the towel. Their energy is sapped, and they don't feel that they have what it takes to overcome the frustration and disappointment. But it is precisely at these moments when we feel that everything is crashing that we need to search for that window of hope and possibility.

Judaism teaches that every great stride in life is preceded by a downfall. The early excitement of a new endeavor is meant to give us a glimpse of what the joy of completion will feel like. But only after the hard work and perseverance that it takes to get there.

This is what is alluded to in the words, "To the land that I will show you." We don't know where the journey will take us. We can and should try to set goals, paint mental pictures, and visualize what we want our life to look like. But we also need to be ready to pivot and readjust and start the journey anew if need be. The one thing that we can be sure of is that we have the inner strength to move forward and the inner wisdom to figure out what our next move should be.

On the very first day of creation, God created a beautiful and powerful inner light and hid it inside of us. It is never extinguished. As we climb our inner ladder using boundless energy, deep love, lifelong learning, and a humble and fearless fire, we have the ability to rediscover the hidden light, impact the world with our brilliance, and reach a state of true spiritual enlightenment.

But it is up to us to take that first step…today!

Like the famous line in *Ethics of Our Fathers*:

> *If I am not for me, who will be for me…and if not now, then when!*

GLOSSARY

binah: understanding; implies a deeper level of understanding, sensing what is being implied rather than just what is being said.

chochmah: wisdom; specifically, information that can be learned and received.

daas: lit., knowledge; often implies a deep experiential knowledge of something and sometimes refers to higher consciousness.

deveikus: connection; cleaving.

emunah: faith, belief.

gematria: the study of numerology.

gevurah: strength, discipline.

hod: splendor.

hispa'alus: awakening to action.

kavod: honor.

kinah: jealousy.

kinyan: transaction.

matzah: unleavened bread.

middos: lit., measurements; used to refer to human attributes and character traits.

midrash: lit., exposition; the texts known as midrash are a collection of early Jewish interpretations of and commentary on the Torah, as taught by the same rabbis who are featured in the Mishnah.

mitzvah: one of the 613 commandments or good deeds related to them.

modeh: thank, praise, admit.

nefesh: life force or spirit; the lowest level of the five soul levels.

neshamah: breath of life; the middle level of the five soul levels.

olam: world.

omein: craftsman or artisan.

p'nim: inner essence.

panim: face.

Talmud: largest and most widely studied compilation of Jewish writings in numerous volumes, in which Jewish law and thought is discussed and debated.

tikkun: repairing of damage.

tikkun olam: repairing the world.

yeshiva: school dedicated to Torah study.

yirah: awe.

zerizus: alacrity, quickness.

BIOGRAPHIES OF AUTHORS AND WORKS QUOTED

Accounting of the Soul: Cheshbon Hanefesh was published in 1809 by Menachem Mendel Levin as a step-by-step program for self-improvement and character refinement. It was republished in 1845 by the students of Rabbi Yisrael Salanter, founder of the *Mussar* movement (see below).

Arizal: Rabbi Isaac Luria (1534–1572), known as the Ari (the Lion), or Arizal (the **Ari,** *zichrono livrachah,* of blessed memory), was a leading rabbi and Kabbalist in the holy city of Safed. Considered the father of contemporary Kabbalah, he gave a new language and presentation to ancient Kabbalistic ideas.

Baal Shem Tov: Rabbi Yisrael Ben Eliezer (1700–1760), known as the Baal Shem Tov (Master of the Good Name), was a Kabbalist and healer who lived in the Ukraine. He is the founder of the Chassidic movement, and his disciples founded the great Chassidic dynasties.

Building a Sanctuary in My Heart: Bilvavi Mishkan Evneh is a series of books detailing practical steps on how to attain the state of feeling connection to God at all times. Originally released in the early 2000s anonymously, the author, Rabbi Itamar Schwartz, has since become a well-known author and lecturer in Israel.

Duties of the Heart: Chovos Halevavos is a famous ethical work by Rabbi Bachya ibn Pakuda (11th century Spain), and translated from Arabic by Chacham Yehudah ibn Tibon, presenting teachings related to Jewish philosophy, spirituality, and ethics.

Ethics of Our Fathers: Pirkei Avos, literally "Chapters of Our Fathers," is a section of the Mishnah, one of the most fundamental works of the Jewish Oral Law, authored in the 3rd century CE. While most of the books of Mishnah focus on Jewish law, *Pirkei Avos* is devoted exclusively to the ethical and moral statements of the Sages.

Maharal: Judah Loew ben Bezalel (1520–1609), known as the Maharal (acronym for Moreinu Harav Loew, our teacher Rabbi Loew), was a renowned mystic, philosopher, and author, who was a leading rabbi in the cities of Mikulov in Moravia and Prague in Bohemia.

Maimonides: Rabbi Moshe Ben Maimon (1135–1204), known by the acronym Rambam, was a Rabbinic authority, philosopher, and doctor in Spain and Egypt. His works, including a codification of the legal content of the Talmud, books on Torah law and Jewish philosophy, and commentary on the classical texts, have been widely studied through the ages.

Nefesh Hachaim: A classic work on the fundamentals of Jewish belief written by Rabbi Chaim of Volozhin (1749–1821), the foremost disciple of the Vilna Gaon and founder of the renowned yeshiva of Volozhin, which became the prototype for the great yeshivas of Eastern Europe.

Noam Elimelech: Rabbi Elimelech of Lizensk (1717–1787), known as the Noam Elimelech, was one of the founding rabbis of the Chassidic movement. *Noam Elimelech* is also the name of the book he authored, which lays out many of the fundamental principles of the Chasidic movement. In 1772 he settled in Lizensk, Galicia, which became an important Chassidic center.

Proverbs: A book in the third section (called *Kesuvim*) of the Hebrew Bible exploring values, morals, and the meaning of life. The Hebrew title is *Mishlei Shlomo*, or *The Proverbs of Solomon*, a reference to King Solomon, who, according to Jewish tradition, is its author.

Rabbi Klonymos Kalman Shapiro (1889–1943): The Rabbi of Piaseczna, Poland, who authored a number of works and was murdered by the Nazis during the Holocaust. Among his many works, the most well-known is *Aish Kodesh* (*The Holy Fire*), which he authored while leading the community in the Warsaw Ghetto.

Rabbi Moshe Chaim Luzzatto (1707–1746): Often referred to as the Ramchal, he was a prominent Italian Jewish rabbi, Kabbalist, and philosopher. He authored many works on ethics, philosophy, and Kabbalah. His works *Path of the Just (Mesilas Yesharim)* and *The Way of God (Derech Hashem)* are quoted throughout this book.

Rabbi Nachman of Breslov (1772–1810): A great-grandson of the Baal Shem Tov, Rabbi Nachman was a Chassidic leader and founder of the Breslov Chassidic movement. He placed great emphasis on joy, happiness, and hope, as well as meditating and having conversations with God while alone in nature. Today, many travel to his grave in Uman, Ukraine, to pray, especially on Rosh Hashanah.

Rashi: Rabbi Shlomo Ben Yitzchak (1040–1104), also known as Rabbi Shlomo Yitzchaki, known by the acronym *Rashi*, was a medieval French rabbi who was the leading commentator on the Bible and Talmud, providing a running commentary that is clear and concise, focusing on the simple interpretation.

Rabbi Tzadok HaKohen Rabinowitz (1823–1900): famed master of Chassidic thought and prolific author in all areas of Judaism, including law, Chassidus, Kabbalah, and ethics. He also wrote scholarly essays on astronomy, geometry, and algebra. He became part of the Chassidic movement as an adult and refused to hold any rabbinic position until late in his life. His work *Tzidkas Hatzaddik* is quoted in this book.

Shulchan Aruch: lit., "the set table"; the most widely consulted of the various legal codes in Judaism. It was authored by Rabbi Yosef Karo in Safed in the 15th century and published in Venice two years later.

The Vilna Gaon: Eliyahu ben Shlomo Zalman Kremer (1720–1797) is known as the Vilna Gaon (the genius from Vilna). He was a Talmudist, halachist, Kabbalist, and one of the foremost leaders of Jewry of the past few centuries. His comments have been published on nearly every one of the classical writings.

ABOUT THE AUTHOR

RABBI SHLOMO BUXBAUM is a passionate Jewish educator, motivational speaker, and life coach in the Greater Washington, DC, area, working with both families and young adults from all different Jewish backgrounds. A student of Yeshivas Toras Moshe and the Mirrer Yeshiva, Rabbi Buxbaum received rabbinic ordination from Aish HaTorah and Rabbi Zalman Nechemia Goldberg, zt"l. Rabbi Buxbaum was the rabbi of Aish HaTorah of Greater Washington for eight years before launching the Lev Experience together with his wife, Devorah, with the mission of empowering individuals to find greater meaning, purpose, and possibilities in life by deepening their connection to Jewish wisdom and values. Rabbi Buxbaum also lectures for various other educational institutions in Maryland and is a frequent scholar-in-residence throughout America. Rabbi Buxbaum, his wife, and their six children live in Silver Spring, Maryland.

Made in the USA
Las Vegas, NV
15 March 2024

87277320R00125